THE
KEY WEST
KEY LIME PIE
COOKBOOK

Barbara –
Love & Limes!

Key West
2015

DAVID L. SLOAN

PHANTOM PRESS
KEYWEST

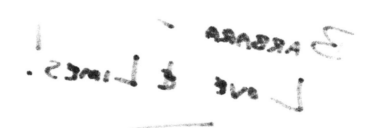

Cover photo: © Heather Smoke
www.curlygirlkitchen.com

Young women pose for photographs during the 1953 Key Lime Festival in Key Largo, Florida. Publication info: Byrum, Joanne / Sweeting, Jackie /Smith, Carolyn /Kaufman, Barbara /Albury, Dorothy. Uncle Johnny. Source: State Archives Of Florida.

3

"Part of the secret of success in life is to eat what you want and let the food fight it out inside."

— Mark Twain

How To Use This Book

Key lime pie is a simple dessert. Recipes have evolved through the years, but the simplicity remains.

- Start by reading the fascinating history of Key lime pie. It really is fascinating.

- Choose a crust. Choose a filling. Choose a sauce. Choose a topping. Make a pie. Each aspect of the pie has its own section with 20 recipe choices.

- Recipes are laid out in a simple, easy to follow format. All you need is a basic understanding of cooking and some tools you probably have in your kitchen already.

- Nutrition facts are provided. Actual numbers will vary depending on the brand you use, but these give a good ballpark figure. Pay attention to what you eat.

- Tips and tricks are provided to give additional insight. They are a quick read and worth checking out before you try a recipe in that section.

- Check out the boxes at the bottoms of the pages. They have fun facts and information you can take as your own.

- If you don't like a recipe, change it. It is difficult to screw up a Key lime pie.

- Have fun. Play some Jimmy Buffett music, drink a margarita, and dance around your kitchen. That's the way we do it in the Florida Keys. (at least I do.)

An Early Native Recipe

Ye Old Conch Recipes

KEY LIME PIE

Condensed milk, egg yolks and lime juice are ingredients of the original Key Lime Pie.

One 15-ounce can sweetened condensed milk.

One-half cup lime juice.

Grated rind of one lime.

Two eggs, separated.

Blend condensde milk with lime juice, grated rind and egg yolks. Beat thoroughly; beat egg whites stiff. Fold into lime mixture. Turn into a baked 8-inch pie shell or Graham cracker crust. Chill well. Makes 8-inch pie.

If desired, egg white may be omitted from filling to make a richer mixture. The egg whites can be used for meringue topping on the pie.

Monroe County Public Library Archives

In The Beginning

Classic Recipes

Just The Crusts

Nothing More Than Fillings

Simply Sauces

No Stopping Toppings

Alternative Pies & More

The Best Key Lime Pie

The Key lime pie: Perhaps no dessert can bring such pleasure to the senses and at the same time spark lively debates, heated arguments and the occasional fistfight.

It is a testament to the dessert that people feel a sense of ownership, even self-righteousness, when it comes to combining a few simple ingredients in their own unique fashion. Carefully guarded recipes have been passed down through generations, with dueling factions each claiming their recipe as the original — and the best. Graham cracker crust versus pastry crust, whipped cream versus meringue and baked versus unbaked are the Hatfield and McCoy feuds of the Key lime pie world. It is a battle with no end in sight, likely to wage on for eternity. The only winners are those of us fortunate enough to be around when a freshly made pie appears. The only losers are the ones who show up after it is gone.

My search for the best Key lime pie revealed that the earliest versions didn't use graham crackers or pastry crust. They didn't have meringue or whipped cream either. Recipes evolved based on tradition, available ingredients and, most importantly, personal preferences — which is what this cookbook is all about. Crusts, fillings, toppings, garnishes, sauces and baking methods each have their own section with tips, tricks and curious bits of information tucked in along the way. There is no wrong way to make a Key lime pie. Simply choose your favorite recipe in each category, mix and match and enjoy. There are over 150,000 pie variations here. Chances are the one you create will be unlike any other. It will probably be the best too. As my friend Tim Watson likes to say, the ultimate Key lime pie, without fail, is *always* the one in front of you.

Real Florida Key lime pie advertised on the wall of John's Store in this 1950's photo from the L.P. Artman Jr. Collection of The Monroe County Public Library Archives. Note the sign in the lower right offering Key limes for sale.

Can Pie Change Your Life?

"Start making Key lime pie and you'll have more time to work on your buns."

Little did I know this advice would lead to a passion, the passion to a profession, and the profession to an obsession. It all started back in August of 1987.

My first job in High School was at Purdy's Restaurant. We served some of the best burgers in Texas and were famous for buns baked fresh on premise. I started as a counter boy — expediting orders, garnishing plates and stocking soda bins. Eventually I moved to the cash register and when opportunity knocked, I'd help out with kitchen prep, bus tables, or jump behind the grill. It didn't matter that I was making $3.35 an hour. I felt alive in the restaurant business, and it beat the hell out of my previous job mowing lawns.

Purdy's stood apart from other burger joints. The black and white checkered floor was lined with oversized booths. A recording with hundreds of hits from the '50's played on a loop. We pioneered the self-serve produce bar and everything was prepared out in the open. People could watch the butcher cutting meat, the cooks working an open grill and the baker mixing dough. In addition to buns, the bakery served old-fashioned candies, fresh baked cookies and, of course, pie. Our clientele was mostly business people.

Our manager believed they were escaping their cubicles for a quick burger and a Vanilla Coke, but I'm still convinced they were there to watch the freak show. We were a unique team of employees at Purdy's and not a one of us was normal.

Ivan was our main baker. He stood just over six feet tall with red hair and forearms that bulged like Popeye's. Ivan was narcoleptic, which meant he would fall asleep sitting down, standing up, in the middle of conversations… pretty much any time. On several occasions customers let us know the baker was sleeping. We would go back to the bakery and find Ivan snoring away at the prep table — dough in hand. At 17 years old, this was the finest entertainment I had seen.

Ivan's naps were brief. He was an excellent baker and the condition rarely affected his work. Even Ivan would joke about his narcolepsy, but it was no laughing matter the morning of his accident. A loud clatter came from the bakery and several of us ran to the back. Ivan was on the floor by the Hobart mixer with a confused look on his face and a wrist the size of a grape fruit. He had fallen asleep on the way to the oven and snapped his wrist in two places. Ivan needed a doctor. Purdy's needed hamburger buns.

"The buns aren't going to bake themselves." My manager said. "How would you like to be a baker, Sloan?"

"I don't know how to bake." I replied.

"It pays six buck an hour." Was his reply.

I told him the buns would be ready in time for lunch.

The next month had me in a literal hot seat. Ruined hamburger and hotdog buns filled the trashcan while oven burns filled my arms. Too much yeast, not enough yeast, over-cooked, under-cooked. You name it, I did it. Besides producing 500 buns a day I had a display case to stock with cookies, brownies and pie. Oven space was at a premium so varied cooking temperatures were out. Pecan Pies burned. Apple Pies exploded. I won't mention The Rum Raison Incident. Every time I baked a batch of pies I fell behind on the buns and it became difficult to hide the fact I was flustered from the 300 lunch patrons who watched on in amusement from the dining room each day. At least the cookies and brownies came out okay.

Quality improved over the next month but I was still running behind. A regular customer approached the bakery counter one afternoon to share some friendly advice.

"Start making Key lime pie and you'll have more time to focus on your buns," she said.

I though she was flirting and blushed.

" I'm sorry?"

"Key lime pie. The recipe is simple and it will free up your ovens." she said.

"That's great advice. Thanks for the suggestion."

"I'm serious. Look up a recipe and you'll see."

I blew off the suggestion, like a good teenager would, and continued to juggle buns, pies and cookies. Several weeks later I was punching in and found a recipe attached to my time card. "Try it! You'll like it!" was written in black, block letters. The note was signed "Judy."

Another month passed before I gave it a try. I'd love to tell you time stood still as the heavens opened up and a bright light shone upon the pie accompanied by a choir of angels. It wasn't such a spectacular event, but I was impressed by the simplicity of the recipe and my boss was pleased with the food cost. I still struggled to keep up with the baking schedule, but the new pie required almost no oven time and I was getting things done a few minutes faster. Perhaps the most rewarding thing about the discovery of Key lime pie was that people loved it! It became a pretty successful item at Purdy's and I continued making them until the day I left for college, clearing the way for a fully recovered Ivan to return.

I enrolled in Florida International University's Hospitality Program in 1989. A slew of cooking classes taught me the science behind the art of baking and I was able to figure out where I had gone wrong with each mistake apart from the Rum Raison Fiasco.

Nepotism landed me a Chef's Apprentice position and I had the great fortune to train under Pascal Oudin at the Coral Gables Colonnade Hotel. Pascal was the best around. He had just been named South Florida's Chef of the year and taught the art behind the science. My fascination with the art and science of everything culinary has continued to grow since, becoming more of a passion than a profession as I ventured into hotel and cruise ship management.

1996 brought me to Key West. I jumped head first into researching the island's haunted history and dug deep into each location. The Curry Mansion had literature claiming to be the birthplace of Key lime pie and I was astounded. Was I really standing in the kitchen where the fist Key lime pie was created? Ghosts were put on the back burner that evening while I tried the recipe myself. Not bad, but I wanted to know more. Why was Key lime pie created in a millionaire's mansion? On an island? In Key West? Who inspired it? How was it originally prepared?

The recipe led me on a quest to verify and recreate the first real Key lime pie. I alone would end a century of debate over graham cracker crust or pastry crust, bake or no bake, whipped cream or meringue. As research continued and answers presented themselves my objective changed. I became obsessed with creating the ultimate Key lime pie.

Over the next decade family and friends were subjected to samplings, questionnaires and blind taste tests. Ingredients were manipulated and the kitchen became a key lime laboratory. I ordered Key lime pie with every meal and soon learned to become a "taster"— limiting myself to one or two bites. I mastered the toppings, aced the garnish and sauces, and excelled with presentation. I tried every cooking method imaginable and did a fine job with crusts and fillings. The pies were excellent but still needed more. Nearly twelve years passed before I stumbled upon the perfect ingredients.

In July of 2008 I created the ultimate Key lime pie. I made several and shared them with friends who confirmed what I hoped was not a figment of my imagination. The pie had perfect crust, filling, topping, garnish, sauce and presentation. Reactions don't lie. Everyone who sampled it was in heaven.

Before you call me a braggart, I should let you know that the ultimate Key lime pie was my creation, not my invention. Servants, chefs, housewives, garden clubs, Conchs and bakers with far more experience did the difficult work. We are simply the fortunate benefactors of a sweet reward.

Read on and you will see that each element of every pie has an art and a science that is yours to manipulate. Create your pies with passion and mix every ingredient with love. Use the techniques that best fit your style and you will come to realize as I did that the main ingredient in the ultimate Key lime pie is You.

Bon Appetite!

David L. Sloan

**Key limes for sale — Fresh from the tree — A dozen for you and a nickel for me
Take 'em to the kitchen — put 'em in a pie — a little slice of heaven, yes, my, oh my!**

A Key lime rhyme passed down through the years. Children in Key West would sell all types of fruit, including limes for extra change. The photo above shows two boys selling Spanish limes on a Key West lane in 1935.

The Fascinating History of Key Lime Pie

Once Upon A Lime...

The Lime Groves Are That-A-Way . . . .

Crusaders waging wars in Palestine were intrigued by the taste of limes and brought them back to Europe.

An early mentor in my Key lime pie research was none other than D.O. Christian Rieger. He wrote The Unusual History of Key Lime Pie and devoted many an hour researching the pie's origins and perfecting his own recipes. The following history is a collaborative effort based on his original writings and research.

Each year Key lime pie climbs in the ranks of America's favorite desserts. It is the official pie of the State of Florida, a staple on nearly every menu from Key West to Florida City, and rapidly appearing in diners and fine restaurants around the world. The pie filling is made with three basic ingredients: eggs, sweetened condensed milk and Key lime juice. The crust and topping are a matter of choice. So what is it that makes this pie so special?

What's in a name?

Key limes are the heart and soul of the Key lime pie. Tart, aromatic and flavorful, the fruit takes its name from crops that once flourished in the Florida Keys. Hurricanes destroyed most of these trees and commercial crops moved south of the border. Ask a Conch (the term for a Key West native) and they will insist the tree must grow in the Florida Keys for her fruit to be considered Key limes. True Key lime trees are mainly found in backyards of Conch homes today, but as the Key lime consistently spikes in popularity, the term is now generally used to describe any lime of the Citrus aurantifolia species, despite where it is grown.

Citrus aurantifolia

Citrus aurantifolia was cultivated for more than a thousand years before reaching the Florida Keys. Native to the Indo-Malayan region of Southeast Asia, it journeyed to the Iberian Peninsula during the crusades and then on to

North Africa and Mediterranean Europe. Christopher Columbus is credited with bringing the fruit to Hispaniola, now Haiti, and Spanish Conquistadors

Early sailors are shown loading limes on a vessel in this clipping from the Monroe County Public Library Archives. The Key lime, or citrus aurantifolia is native to the Indo-Malayan region of Southeast Asia.

introduced it to the United States. By 1520 the lime was commonly grown in Haiti. Key lime crops were reported as "increasing" in Florida by 1839, though the exact date of introduction is unknown. Of all limes it has been the longest known and most widely cultivated.

Size Matters

Key limes are about the size of a golf ball, usually an inch in diameter, but may be slightly smaller or larger. Thin-skinned and yellow when ripe, they are nearly spherical with a greenish, yellow pulp and many seeds. It is smaller and juicier than larger hybrids and the fresh fruit can be kept refrigerated for several weeks. The skin may turn leathery-looking and tan, but it will still be juicy and tasty on the inside. The Key lime tree is thorny, making it hazardous to reach into to pick fruit. This is just as well, as the limes drop to the ground where they can be easily collected when their peak flavor is reached.

Location, Location, Location

Key West and the Florida Keys are not the place of choice for farming. As chance has conspired, one of the few trees that thrive in this soil and dry climate is the Key lime. Key lime trees grow all over the tropical Western Hemisphere including the West Indies, Central America, and Mexico. The tree yields best in areas where rain exceeds 80 inches a year, yet it tolerates drought better than any other citrus, which explains the wide range of its habitat throughout the tropical world. The tree does well under stress, which explains why it flourishes in the Keys where rainfall averages 23 inches a year. Many natives of the Florida Keys, or Conchs, believe a fruitless tree will produce fruit if it is severely beaten. Loss of leaves generally results in abundant fruit. It is a very productive tree, bearing fruit most of the year. Some years it blooms and bears more than others, but one can usually find fruit on it. Continuous yield and easy harvest explain why it is the most widely grown commercial lime crop in the world. It is widely planted in tropical and semitropical countries for fresh fruit and also for juice export. In 1986 there were 2,000,000 seedlings planted near Colima, in southwest Mexico. Rose's Sweetened Lime Juice is made with these little limes, although clarification and sweetening severely alter the flavor.

The Persian Diversion

The lime most common in grocery stores is the Persian lime. It differs from a Key lime in the most important way; it is a different variety — Citrus latifolia. The Persian lime is two to three times larger than the Key lime, and it does not have as strong a flavor and aroma. It came into Europe from Persia, hence the name, and is a hybrid. No one is sure if the Persians or others bred it. In the United States it grows mostly in Florida where it arrived in 1883.

Why do we use it?

So why do we use Key lime juice instead of the other lime juice for pie? One answer is tradition. Another reason is convenience; as that is what Key Westers grow. Undoubtedly, though, the best reason is the Key lime is more flavorful in cooking than the other limes, and no matter where you enjoy them today, the smell and taste sparks a feeling that is unquestionably 'Florida Keys'. But what about the rest of the pie? Each ingredient contains its own fascinating history and secrets; one created to suppress sexual urges and another inspired by the death of children. Things are heating up in Key lime pie land.

Nov. 11, 1966

Green Key Lime Pie? -- NEVER!

Gail Borden, The Alamo & Condensed Milk

In the next phase of Key lime pie's creation we meet Gail Borden Jr. (1801-1874), a 19th Century American Renaissance man whose name would go on to be synonymous with milk.

Borden was a surveyor, newspaper editor, writer and inventor. He prepared the first topographical map of Texas, surveyed and designed Galveston, Texas, and laid out the City of Houston. With his brother Tom he co-founded Texas' first newspaper, the Telegraph and Texas Land Register, serving as editor. At this job, historians credit him with creating the headline "Remember the Alamo."

Borden helped write Texas' first state constitution, invented the lazy Susan, and adopted the Conestoga Wagon into what became known as the Prairie Schooner. He created the dairy company Borden, and Borden, Texas, is named after him. But it was through his sympathetic quality and his skill as an inventor that he made the most important contribution to the creation of Key lime pie.

By 1853 Borden had experimented with condensing meat and mixing it with biscuits as a wholesome, long-lasting food. For this accomplishment, England gave him an award at a ceremony in London. On his return boat trip from London, he saw several babies die from drinking unwholesome milk provided by on-board cows and realized the need for clean, wholesome milk in a world where dirty people kept dirty cows and produced dirty milk. After lengthy experimentation he received a patent in 1856 for a process by which milk was heated in a vacuum and condensed. The process reduced the volume

by 65 to 80 percent and left behind a milk product rich in solids and milk fat. This is what makes the product particularly delicious. To this he added sugar, which inhibited the growth of bacteria, thus acting as a preservative and the result was a nutritional milk product with a long shelf life — sweetened condensed milk.

The product was delectable — all by itself, straight out of the can. Sweetened condensed milk was diluted to feed babies and ultimately used in desserts. In 1858 Borden founded the New York Condensed Milk Company selling his product on the streets of New York. In the following years he opened several more plants which produced Eagle Brand® sweetened condensed milk.

Borden insisted that the farms that supplied him be clean, an unusual request in his day. To accomplish this, he educated dairy farmers on how to maintain high standards of hygiene, rules which

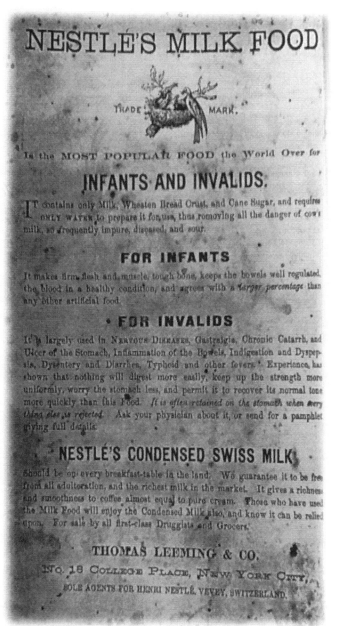

evolved into the sanitary practices of today's dairy industry and were the founding principles of today's local health codes.

Although production was good, the business was not a booming success. Then came the Civil War. Because his canned milk did not need refrigeration, had a long shelf life, and leveled out the seasonal imbalance of milk production, it was ideal for the army — so much so in fact, that they commandeered the company's entire production. After the war, Borden had a ready market from former Northern and Southern soldiers.

Early advertisements for condensed milk promoted benefits for infants and invalids *(left)*. A Spanish ad from the 1890's offers condensed milk for sale at Mr. Recio's store on Duval Street in Key West *(previous page)*. Monroe County Public Library Archives.

Sylvester Graham, Sexual Urges & Graham Crackers

The Reverend Sylvester Graham (1794–1851) was a popular orator and an American health reformer who lectured throughout the eastern United States in the early 1800s and was probably the first person in the United States to lecture about good eating habits to produce good health. He attended Amherst College in Massachusetts and later became a school teacher, but his poor health cut short this career. Afterwards, he became a Presbyterian minister and a member of the Pennsylvania Temperance Society. In these capacities he lectured against alcoholic drink and the evils that accompanied it.

The effects of alcohol on the human body, and his own poor health, led Graham to study anatomy and the effects of alcohol and other substances on the body. Soon he expanded his temperance lectures and began preaching against "venereal excess" or "aching sensibility." Graham felt that intense physical desire, even if you were married, had dire consequences. To control lust he prescribed a special vegetarian diet. He frequently preached before large crowds in hotel auditoriums. Outside, bakers could be found picketing against him.

What could the minister possibly have said to offend these hard-working citizens? Among other things, he preached eating homemade, coarsely ground, whole-grain bread to control venereal excess and because white-flour bread had most of the healthful benefits removed. Since the bakers were baking only with white flour, they felt he threatened their income. But a few of the smart ones came around to his way of thinking — kind of.

They decided if the coarsely ground whole wheat bread had a market among his followers, they could make a buck or two by supplying them with it. And these smart guys called the flour they used "Graham flour" after the minister who was trying to make his listeners more health conscious and less lustful. Graham flour had been around for a long time before this but had remained nameless. It differs from whole–wheat flour in that it is more coarsely ground. In 1829 Graham created a recipe for a healthy cracker. This, his followers and the bakers dubbed the "Graham Cracker." In 1898 Nabisco became the first commercial baker to introduce the product nationwide.

Graham cracker crumbs are the main ingredients in the crust of many classic Key lime pie recipes. Little did the Reverend Sylvester Graham know his crackers would one day become an integral part in the symphony of flavors in a dessert of which he would not have approved. In the late 1800s Will K. and Dr. John Harvey Kellogg would create the massive breakfast cereal industry. One can trace its beginnings back to the work of this dedicated minister, the Reverend Sylvester Graham.

And Then Along Comes Sally?

Aunt Sally is credited as the inventor of the Key lime pie. The problem is no one seems to know who she was. Most accounts agree that she was a cook at the Curry Mansion in Key West where she created the pie, but from that point, her identity has been anyone's guess.

William Curry was Florida's first millionaire. He made his fortune with a chandlery, supplying ships with goods and hardware. Sweetened condensed milk was popular with the shipping community given its nutrition, and long shelf life, so it is only logical this would be a product William Curry carried. In fact, records from 1918 show him paying $2381.40 to the Borden Condensed Milk Co. This was certainly not his first order, but the earliest from surviving records. It would make sense that he brought a few cans of the product back to his home for the cooks to experiment with, but who was Aunt Sally? We can start our search in 1856.

1856 was the year Gail Borden received his patent for sweetened condensed milk. According to Florida Keys historian, Tom Hambright, the first known published reference to Key lime pie appeared in a 1930s WPA promotion and advertised "World Famous Key Lime Pie." Key West cookbooks prior to this had no mention of the pie. That leaves a seventy year period where Aunt Sally could have existed. Searches of the census show no one named Sally associated with the Curry family, but the 1910 census contains records for two women named Sally. The first is Sally Miliken, a white woman born in 1844 who hailed from Illinois. It is unknown when she came to Key West. The second is Sally Deaveroux, a black woman born in 1871 in the West Indies. She immigrated to Key West in 1898. Could Sally

Deaveroux be the Aunt Sally? Possibly, but the recipe at the Curry Mansion says the real Aunt Sally cooked at the home in 1894. If this date is correct, it would rule out Sally Deaveroux.

Which leads us to Sarah Jane Lowe. Sarah's parents were from the Bahamas. The 1885 census shows her living in Key West, not only close to the Curry Mansion, but married to William Curry's son Charles who was a clerk at his father's chandlery. William had nine children and seventeen grandchildren. Sally is a nickname for Sarah, just as Bill is to William or Bob to Robert. This would leave fourteen of William Curry's grandchildren referring to Sarah Jane Lowe as "Aunt Sally". Though she would clearly not have been employed as a cook at the mansion, the possibility exists that her name could be attached to the pie. But even if Sarah Jane Lowe is the elusive Aunt Sally, she may not be the Key lime pie's originator.

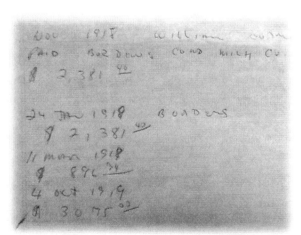 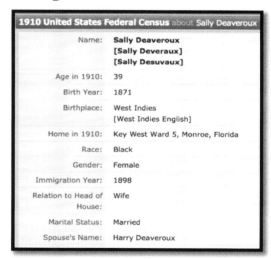

1910 United States Federal Census about Sally Deaveroux	
Name:	**Sally Deaveroux** **[Sally Deveraux]** **[Sally Desuvaux]**
Age in 1910:	39
Birth Year:	1871
Birthplace:	West Indies [West Indies English]
Home in 1910:	Key West Ward 5, Monroe, Florida
Race:	Black
Gender:	Female
Immigration Year:	1898
Relation to Head of House:	Wife
Marital Status:	Married
Spouse's Name:	Harry Deaveroux

William Curry's payments to the Borden's Condensed Milk Company noted above (left) indicate large volumes of the product were purchased for his chandlery in Key West. The 1910 Federal Census (right) identifies Sally Deaveroux, a possible 'Aunt Sally' candidate. The 1885 Census on the following page identifies Sarah Jane Lowe (Curry) as a more likely candidate.

Page No. 40

Supervisor's Dist. No. 3

Enumeration Dist. No. 4

Note A.—The Census Year begins June 1, 1884, and ends May 31, 1885.
Note B.—All persons will be included in the Enumeration who were living on the 1st day of June, 1885. No others will. Children BORN SINCE June 1, 1885, will be OMITTED. Members of Families who have DIED SINCE June 1, 1885, will be INCLUDED.
Note C.—Questions Nos. 10, 14, 22 and 23 are not to be asked in respect to persons under 10 years of age.

SCHEDULE 1.—Inhabitants in _Key West_, in the County of _Monroe_, State of _Florida_

enumerated by me on the _twenty-sixth_ day of June, 1885.

Lafayette Lowe, Enumerator.

			Name of each Person whose place of abode on 1st June, 1885, was in this family.					Civil Condition			Occupation		Education		Nativity		
	40 52		Peter Porter	M B 24		Servant					Cook				Florida	Florida	Florida
			Caroline Holbert	F B 30							Clerk				Bahamas	Bahamas	Bahamas
	40 53		W A Lowe	M W 32											do	do	do
			Caroline Lowe	F W 42		Wife									do	do	do
			Virginia Lowe	F W 16		Daughter									Florida	do	do
			Augusta Lowe	F W 7		do									do	do	do
	40 54		Lydia Lowe	F W 13										1	do	do	do
			Harley Curry	M W 39							Clerk				do	do	do
			Sarah Curry	F W 34		Wife									do	Florida	Florida
			Walter Curry	M W 11		Son								1	do	do	do
			Louise Curry	F W 9		Daughter								1	do	do	do
			Winton Curry	M W 5		Son									do	do	do
			Sophia Curry	F W 3		Daughter									do	do	do
			Dulia Alexander	F B 35		Servant	1					Cook Laundress			1 1	Bahamas	Bahamas	Bahamas
	40 55		William Edwicks	M W 40				1			Fisherman				Hungary	Hungary	Hungary
			Louisa Edwicks	F W 30		Wife									Florida	England	Bahamas
			Katie Edwicks	F W 10		Daughter								1	do	Florida	Florida
			Louis F Edwicks	M W 7		Son									do	Florida	
			Eddie Edwicks	M W 3		do									do	do	
	40 56		William Curry	M W 42				1			Merchant				Bahamas	Bahamas	do
			Sophia Curry	F W 40		Wife									do	do	do
			Tessie Curry	F W 20		Daughter									Florida	do	do
			Walter Curry	M W 18		Son					Clerk				do	do	do
			John McGinnis	M W 24		Servant		1			Groceryboy			1 1	do	do	do
			Priscilla Campbell	F B 26		do					House servant				do	do	do
	40 57		George W Patterson	M W 45							Lawyer				Belgium	Belgium	Bahamas
			— Patterson	F W 37		Wife									Belgium	Belgium	Bahamas
			Lizzie Patterson	F W 17		Daughter								1	Florida	Florida	do
			May Patterson	F W 13		do									do	do	do
			Ella Patterson	F W 11		do									do	do	do
			Patrician Patterson	F W 8		do									do	do	do
			Sarah Patterson	F W 77		Mother		1							do	do	do
			Susan Stocker	F B 40		Sister		1							do	Conn	Ga
			Georgia Stocker	F B 3		Niece									Georgia	Georgia	Florida
			Edgar Stocker	M B 40		Brother									Florida	Ga	do
			Otto Matlock	M W 41		Nephew			1						Key West	New York	New York
			Andrew Beasley	F B 16		Servant								1 1	Florida	Norfolk	Florida
	40 58		John Lowe	M W 62											Bahamas	Bahamas	Bahamas
			Augusta Lowe	F W 53		Wife		1							do	do	do
			Geo H Lowe	M W 22		Son		1			Farmer				Florida	do	do
	40 59		Simon Machetavich	M W 32				1							Key West	Ghent	Machetavich
			Nye Machetavich	F W 27		Wife		1							Cuba	Cuba	Cuba
			Julia Machetavich	F W 4		Daughter									Florida	New York	do
			Rufa Machetavich	F W 3		do									do	do	do
			Alfred Machetavich	M W 1		Son									do	do	do
			Washington Machetavich	M B 16		Brother		1			Cook				Africa	Africa	Venezuela
			Maria Saunders	F B 18		Servant		1						1 1	Bahamas	Bahamas	Bahamas
			Virginie Claro	F W 78		do		1			Nurse				do	do	do
	57 60		Enrique Madan	M W 28				1			Cigar Maker				Cuba	Cuba	Cuba

Note D.—In making entries in columns 9, 10, 11, 12, 19 to 23, an affirmative mark only will be used—thus / ; except in the case of divorced persons, column 11, when the letter "D" is to be used.
Note E.—Question No. 12 will only be asked in cases where an affirmative answer has been given either to question 10 or to question 11.
Note F.—Question No. 14 will only be asked in cases where a gainful occupation has been reported in column 15.
Note G.—In column 7 an abbreviation for the name of the month may be used, as Jan., Apr., Dec.

35

Aunt Sally's
KEY LIME PIE

**Key Lime Pie was first created in this house by Aunt Sally,
a cook who worked for the Curry family in 1894**

INGREDIENTS
4 eggs separated
1/2 cup key lime juice
14-ounce can sweetened condensed milk
1/3 cup sugar
pinch of cream of tartar
1 graham cracker crust 8"

DIRECTIONS
Beat egg yolks until light and thick. Blend in lime juice, then milk, stirring until mixture thickens. Pour mixture into pie shell. Beat egg whites with cream of tartar until stiff. Gradually beat in sugar, beating until glossy peaks form. Spread egg whites over surface of pie to edge of crust. Bake in 350° oven until golden brown, about 20 minutes. Chill before serving.

Hookers, Sponges & The First Key Lime Pie

Key West historian, Tom Hambright, has his own theory about the origins of Key lime pie. He believes it was a creation concocted by sponge fisherman.

Sponge harvesting started in the Florida Keys as early as the 1820s when local fishermen discovered sponges washed up on the beach after storms. An industry was formed and 'hookers,' as they were called because of their method for harvesting sponges, set out on small skiffs for several days at a time. Sweetened condensed milk would have been a staple on their boats in the late 1800s, as would Key limes. Hambright believes the spongers collected wild bird eggs from the out islands, combined them with the other ingredients on board and a pie was born. Key West extreme chef, author and adventurer Paul Menta tracked down the oldest hookers he could find to confirm the theory. During his quest he confirmed sweetened condensed milk was brought to the sponge fields to mix with coffee, but more interestingly, that Cuban bread was soaked in the condensed milk as it started to go stale. The mixture was topped with whatever eggs were around. Wild bird, turtle — everything was fair game. Lime was squeezed on top to cook the mixture as you would a ceviche, and a Key lime pie was born. Most sponge fishermen were black at the time. Hambright reasons one of the spongers was associated with a cook at the Curry Mansion. The concept traveled from water to land and began to evolve. Menta believes the pie may have been considered a lower class food in the beginning. This could explain why it didn't appear in cookbooks for many years. Another possibility is there was no reason to include the recipe, as it was so simple to remember.

```
Hooker Style Key Lime Pie (serves 2)

1 can Eagle Brand sweetened condensed milk
2 Key limes
1 egg yolk (save the white for breakfast as nothing's wasted on the boat)
6 inches stale Cuban bread loaf
2 coffee cups
1 spoon

Break up some stale bread, the real hard stuff and put enough in the
coffee cups to cover bottom. Pour about an ounce of sweet milk in the
bottom of each cup. Take the can of sweet milk and squeeze both limes in
it until they are dry, drop egg yolk in can and mix like crazy with your
spoon. Pour equal amounts in each cup, top with more bread and let sit out
in the sun for 5 hours. After jelly setting has appeared, eat and enjoy.
```

A sponge fisherman or "hooker" Key lime pie recipe courtesy of Extreme Chef Paul Menta. This is likely how the first Key lime pie was prepared. Hookers often prepared the dish in the sweetened condensed milk can, but the practice has risks mixing acidic lime with the can's metal.

In 1905 there was at least one commercial Key lime grove in the Upper Keys. Most of the farming at that time was pineapples and tomatoes. Henry Flagler started shipping less expensive Cuban pineapples around 1912, paving the way for Key lime crops where the pineapples were once grown and saving us all from eating Key Pineapple Pie on a stick today. By 1917 there were 183 acres of Key lime groves in the Upper Keys. 60,000 crates of limes were shipped that year. When the first Overseas Highway opened in 1928, land became more valuable for development than farming. Canals dug to drain the Everglades lowered the water table more than five feet adding additional hardships, and the less expensive Persian lime was introduced to Florida. Charter fishing became a more lucrative business for many farmers, and by 1931 only 10,000 crates of Key limes were shipped. The 1935 hurricane delivered the final blow to the Florida Keys commercial Key lime crop. If you live in the Florida Keys and are reading this, plant a few Key lime trees in your yard to ensure our backyard crops continue to thrive.

Monroe County Public Library Archives

An individual prunes Key lime trees in Upper Matacumbe Key in this 1919 photograph from the State Archives of Florida, JK Small Collection. The 1935 hurricane marked the end of commercial lime crops in the Keys with the exception of one man on Elliot Key who continued until 1960. His was the last commercial lime crop to exist in the Florida Keys.

Native Recipes Through The Years

.

Pies

"An ounce of good practical experience is often worth a pound of theory, and the most perfect recipe will fail if its ingredients are not put together properly."

PUMPKIN PIE FILLING

Filling for three pies. One quart can pumpkin; one large can cream; one small can cream; one can condensed milk; one condensed milk can water; six eggs; one and one-half teaspoon cornstarch. Combine ingredients.

MRS. MEARS.

LEMON PIE

One-half package Uneeda Crackers; one pint boiling water; yolk of one or two eggs; one cup sugar; two lemons (juice) salt. Pour water on cracker crumbs (roll crackers fine). Let cool; beat in eggs, sugar and add juice. Use egg whites for meringue.

Lemon pie was a predecessor of the Key Lime pie. Above is an early recipe from a Key West Cook Book. Crusts made from Uneeda Crackers, ® were standard for many Conch Key lime pie recipes. This recipe was located in The Monroe County Public Library Archives.

The history of the little yellow Key Lime is quite interesting to the people of the Mainland. During the days of sailing ships and pirates, the seeds were brought to the Keys by sailors, and planted where-ever they found fresh water. Limes were used in those days to prevent scurvy, on their long voyages. On their return trips, they would gather the limes along with the water. The early settlers from the Bahamas also brought with them the Key Lime seeds, from which groves were started from Key West to Key Largo. Limes grown on the Florida Keys have a distinct flavor all their own. The roots reaching down into the brackish water, gives them a tang no other lime seems to have, and its delightful to the taste. Though they are not as plentiful as they used to be, we manage to keep a supply, so we can make our Key Lime Pie the year round.

Key Lime Pie
(Specialty of Pigeon Patio)

4 eggs separated
1 cup sugar
1 tablespoon gelatine - in half cup ice water
½ cup lime juice
½ teaspoon salt

Beat egg yolks till thick, add ½ cup sugar to eggs slowly while beating, add salt then lime juice, beat well. Cook in double boiler about ten minutes or until mixture is thick. Remove cooked mixture to mixing bowl, and add gelatine, beat for about five minutes. Set aside to cool. Beat egg whites very stiff, add sugar and beat till you have a satin smooth consistency. With wooden fork beat in egg whites to cooked mixture, until all is well blended, and there are no lumps of egg white. Pour into baked 9" pie shell, and either freeze for future use, or chill in refrigerator.

COMMANDER WALTER S. GINN, USN (Ret.) presents Key lime pie to his friend, Mr. Arthur Eyles, at their recent meeting in Los Angeles. Mr. Eyles is the manager of the Prudential Insurance Department, Hawaiian Islands, and is widely known among service men, having served many years as an executive in the Navy YMCA in Honolulu, T. H. Commander Ginn came to Key West for duty from Pearl Harbor after the beginning of the war. He is now retired.

The specialty Key lime pie of Pigeon Patio (left) describes settlers planting Key lime seeds near fresh water to retrieve on their return. The 1948 photo (above) shows Commander Walter S. Ginn of Key West presenting Key lime pie to Arthur Eyles. Eyles claimed no dessert could come close to the laulau of Hawaii. When Commander Ginn told him Key lime pie was served at The Little White House, Eyles insisted on trying it. (Documents courtesy of Monroe County Public Library.

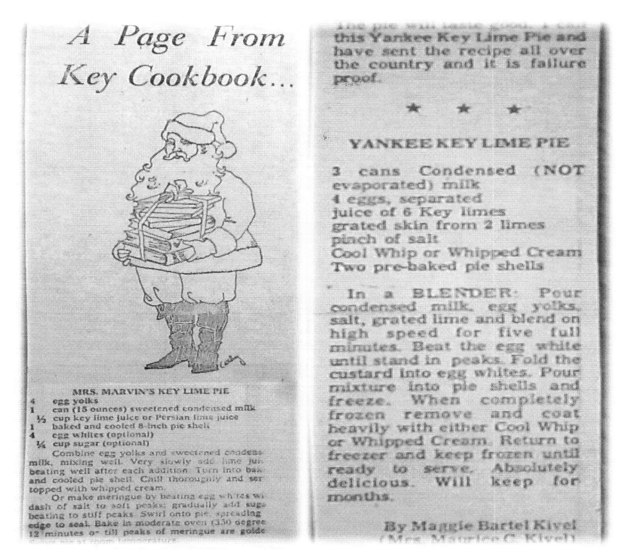

A Page From Key Cookbook...

MRS. MARVIN'S KEY LIME PIE

4   egg yolks
1   can (15 ounces) sweetened condensed milk
½   cup key lime juice or Persian lime juice
1   baked and cooled 8-inch pie shell
4   egg whites (optional)
¼   cup sugar (optional)

Combine egg yolks and sweetened condensed milk, mixing well. Very slowly add lime juice beating well after each addition. Turn into baked and cooled pie shell. Chill thoroughly and serve topped with whipped cream.

Or make meringue by beating egg whites with dash of salt to soft peaks; gradually add sugar beating to stiff peaks. Swirl onto pie, spreading edge to seal. Bake in moderate oven (350 degree) 12 minutes or till peaks of meringue are golden.

The pie will taste good. I eat this Yankee Key Lime Pie and have sent the recipe all over the country and it is failure proof.

★   ★   ★

YANKEE KEY LIME PIE

3 cans Condensed (NOT evaporated) milk
4 eggs, separated
juice of 6 Key limes
grated skin from 2 limes
pinch of salt
Cool Whip or Whipped Cream
Two pre-baked pie shells

In a BLENDER: Pour condensed milk, egg yolks, salt, grated lime and blend on high speed for five full minutes. Beat the egg white until stand in peaks. Fold the custard into egg whites. Pour mixture into pie shells and freeze. When completely frozen remove and coat heavily with either Cool Whip or Whipped Cream. Return to freezer and keep frozen until ready to serve. Absolutely delicious. Will keep for months.

By Maggie Bartel Kivel (Mrs. Maurice C. Kivel)

Two early recipes discovered as clippings in the archives of The Monroe County Public Library, Maggie Kivel's Yankee Key Lime Pie with a whipped cream topping and Mrs. Marvin's Key Lime Pie with a meringue. Each contains their own tips for the perfect pie.

Mrs. Gene Otto keeps house in the home on Eaton St. in which her husband was born. Her kitchen has two ranges ("I never have enough burners on one," she said), copper molds and cabinet doors decorated by her husband. He is a well-known artist.

Her cookery style is Conch and Cuban with French touches learned when they lived in Paris.

Mrs. Otto also is a master at streamlining old recipes. Her doctored b o t t l e d mayonnaise tastes like homemade French or Spanish mayonnaise. She uses canned roast beef in Ropa Vieja.

She learned to make lime pie from her late mother-in-law.

"Gene's mother always s a i d four eggs for family, six for company," said Ann Otto.

Key Lime Pie

6 egg yolks, beaten slightly
1 can sweetened condensed milk
   Juice of 7 large key limes
   (about ½ cup)
1 9-inch baked pie shell
6 egg whites
12 tablespoons sugar

Combine egg yolks and condensed milk and mix well. Add lime juice and blend well. Turn into pie shell. Bake in a moderate oven (350 degrees) until set, about 10 to 15 minutes. Meanwhile beat egg whites until stiff. Gradually beat in sugar and beat until very stiff. Put on pie by large spoonfuls, spreading to edge of pie shell all around. Place in hot oven (400 degrees) for 5 minutes. Reduce heat to 300 degrees and bake until meringue is pale honey colored.

Annette Otto was a concert pianist turned homemaker, and wife of famed Key West Artist Gene Otto. They are remembered today as the owners of Robert, the haunted doll, but those close to Anne knew her for her considerable cooking skills. Anne's spirit is said to haunt The Artist House where she lived. When I dropped her recipe by the guesthouse and suggested we recreate it, the room filled with a sweet perfume scent. Perhaps Anne is still hungry for one of her favorites. Her recipe was adapted from Gene's mother, Minnie Otto. Note the instructions: Four eggs for family, six for company. (Monroe County Public Library Archives)

44

A Monroe Landmark Is This Lime Packing Shed on Key Largo

The clipping above shows a lime packing shed on Key Largo, a reminder of the days when Key limes were a commercial crop in the Florida Keys. On the following page is a native recipe from Merili McCoy. Merili was an activist for many causes in the Florida Keys and went on to serve as a Key West City Commissioner for many years. She was passionate about the future and the past of the Florida Keys. Notice how the article mentions she knew the ingredients by heart. Both clippings are from the Monroe County Public Library Archives.

The filling is top secret. But here's another hint from Cell: if you want a firm, well set filling that slices easily, freeze it overnight. And never use green food coloring.

Her topping is whipped cream, because it's "more popular, and I freeze the pies for wholesale."

Merili McCoy has lived in Key West since childhood and is actively involved in community improvements. When a luncheon conversation turned to desserts, she mentioned that she had a great recipe for real Key lime pie. She's obviously made quite a few of these - she knew the ingredients by heart:

Merili McCoy's Key lime pie

■ Ingredients:
1 prepared graham cracker crust filling
1/2 cup of Key lime juice
1 14-oz can of sweetened condensed milk
4-5 egg yolks (use 4 egg yolks for an 8 inch pie, 5 egg yolks for a 9' pie)
1 tablespoon sugar

■ Meringue:
4-5 egg whites, as above
use 3 tablespoons sugar per egg white
■ Instructions:
1. Separate the eggs. Blend the egg yolks well with the sweetened condensed milk. Add 1 tablespoon sugar and blend. Add the Key lime juice, mix until well blended.
2. To make the meringue, beat the egg whites, along with three tablespoons sugar per egg white, until fluffy and stiff. (Merili's advice: You've beaten the egg whites long enough if they won't slide when the bowl is tilted. They are thoroughly beaten when they won't fall out of an inverted bowl.)
3. Pour the filling into a prepared graham cracker crust, and top with the meringue, sealing the meringue to the edges of the pie.
4. Bake the pie 10-15 minutes in a pre-heated 350 degree oven until the meringue is browned.
If you choose to serve your pie without meringue, bake 10 minutes at 325 degrees.
Another hint from Merili: As you squeeze the juice from the limes, be careful not to include the oil from the skin of the fruit. It will leave a bitter aftertaste. To counteract this, try adding one tablespoon bottled lime juice to your mixture.
■ A few parting tips for your Key lime pie recipe file:
1. If you prefer a graham cracker crust, do not pre-bake it. Fill the formed pie shell and then bake the shell and the filling together, to prevent over-browning.
2. Use your microwave to easily extract the juice from your Key limes. Zap them on high for about 30 seconds — they'll be warm to the touch, and will squeeze easily and yield more juice.
3. Use real Key limes, available from local produce markets and kind neighbors, or use bottled Key lime juice. Lime juice is not Key lime juice. Key limes have been left to ripen and turn yellow on their tree, and have a sweeter, less acidic taste.

Lime Pie

Bake shell of graham cracker or regular pie crust, cool.

1 to 1½ cans of thick condensed milk

3 to 5 eggs, separated

½ cup of Key Limes if possible. It will not be authentic or have the same flavor with other limes.

Beat yolks of eggs until light, add condensed milk and blend well. Add lime juice and blend again. Beat egg whites with ¼ teaspoon of cream of tartar until foamy, continue beating until stiff but not dry, adding one tablespoon of sugar to each egg while beating with rotary or electric beater. Add ¼ teaspoon of vanilla to egg white mixture, and blend about one quarter of mixture with custard. Cover top of pie with balance of egg whites and brown in oven. This is all the cooking necessary - the lime juice cooks the egg and milk.

Cool thoroughly and serve.

KEY LIME PIE

1 can sweetened condensed milk

½ cup lime juice with grated rind of one lime

3 eggs

Separate eggs and beat yolks together with lime juice and sweetened condensed milk. Use dover egg beater and beat until thick. Whip whites until stiff and carefully fold into first mixture. Pour filling into already prepared pie shell and place in refrigerator for several hours before serving. Serve with whipped cream.

Key Lime Pie New York Style

NEW YORK (UPI) — Persian limes, the variety carried by supermarkets across the country, can be used instead of the little yellow Florida Key limes for Key lime pie. Prepare and bake a 9-inch pie crust or crumb crust. Let cool. Finely grate 2 teaspoons of the green peel from a lime and reserve. Squeeze enough limes to measure one-half cup juice. Stir the juice, half the reserved peel and 3 egg yolks into contents of 1 14- or 15-ounce can of sweetened condensed milk until mixture is thick and evenly colored. Beat one egg white until stiff but not dry and fold into the milk mixture to lighten it. Reserve remaining egg whites for other uses. Chill pie well and serve with whipped cream topping lightly sprinkled with the remaining grated peel. Makes six servings.

Pie recipes through the years used different techniques. On this page are three very different recipes from The Monroe County Library Archives. One uses egg whites in the filling, another (for New York Style Key Lime Pie) suggests Persian limes are acceptable, and the recipe above specifies the pie will not be authentic or have the same flavor with other limes. The photo on the following page shows the Sunset Cove Tea Room with a sign indicating tea was not their best seller.

The Sunset Cove Tea Room in Key Largo, 1952 from the State Archives of Florida, Charles Baron Collection.

Mrs. Curry Bakes Best Lime Pie In Keys Contest

Mrs. Elizabeth Curry of Key Largo was judged the best key lime pie baker in Southeast Florida Friday.

She won the grand prize, an electric roaster, in the lime pie baking contest of the Upper Keys Lime Festival. Her pie recipe contains six eggs, one and a half cans of sweetened condensed milk and one-third cup key lime juice.

It can be argued that more eggs make for a tastier pie, as seen in Elizabeth Curry's award winning recipe above. A 1988 Key West Woman's Club recipe (right) from Lorine Thompson includes unflavored gelatin and Angustura bitters, but leaves the choice of crust up to the baker. The variety of Key lime pie recipes published through the years show all types of ingredients and techniques have been used, and all claim to be delicious. (Monroe County Public Library Archives)

Key Lime Pie

The 1988 Key West Woman's Club Cookbook featured this recipe from Lorine Thompson. It's truly delicious!

1 tablespoon unflavored gelatin
1/2 cup cold water
4 eggs, separated
1 cup sugar
1/2 cup fresh lime juice
1/2 teaspoon salt
1 tablespoon Angustura bitters
Grated peel of 1 lime
1 9-inch baked pie crust
Whipped cream for topping

Place the gelatin in the cold water and let it dissolve.

In a separate bowl, beat together the egg yolks, half the sugar, lime juice, and salt. Cook in a double boiler until the mixture coats a spoon. Remove from heat. Add the gelatin mixture; add the bitters and lime peel. Mix well until the mixture begins to thicken. Beat the egg whites and the other half of the sugar until stiff peaks form.

Fold into the egg yolk mixture. Pour into the baked pie crust. Chill. Spread with whipped cream just before serving.

Mary Uhler began selling her Key lime pies in 1954. She credits practice and timing for her reputation as the pie champion. This clipping from the Monroe County Public Library Archives described her Plantation Key store as an icon to piedom.

```
KEY LIME PIE          NO BAKE RECIPE

4 egg yolks
4 egg whites
1 can condensed milk
½ cup fresh lime juice (this may be too tart - it is wise to use to taste)
Whip egg yolk in an electric mixer until thick and lemon colored, the
    longer they are whipped the better.
Add condensed milk to the beaten yolks, but not as high speed
Add lime juice to the egg and milk mixture
Beat egg whites until stiff and folk into mixture
Turn into a baked pie crust, or graham cracker crust and freeze
The pie may be served with a whipped cream topping


Traditional-Baked Meringue
Note: If meringue is desired, then whip the four egg whites until
they form peaks, spread over pie and brown in an oven 350 degrees
until brown.  1 teaspoon sugar to each egg white.  Also add 1
teaspoon cream of tartar to meringue.  Do not freeze.
Baked pie crust or graham cracker crust can be used.


                              May Hill Russell recipe
```

A No Bake Key Lime Pie recipe from May Hill Russell found in the Monroe County Public Library Archives. Pies containing eggs are baked today due to Salmonella risks. Eggs must reach 160°F to kill Salmonella. Pasteurized eggs can still be used to create a no bake pie.

Key lime pie tarts being sold to benefit the Monroe County Special Olympics in this 1977 photo from the State Archives of Florida, Tom McLendon collection.

Just Crusts

Crumb Crust Tips & Tricks

- Resist premade and store bought crusts. The crust recipes in the book are quick, simple and preservative free.

- For a coarser crust, place your grahams, cookies, cereal or nuts in a one gallon freezer bag and crush with a rolling pin or wine bottle. For a finer crust, use a food processor.

- Use a little butter or non-stick spray on your pans, even if the pans are non-stick.

- Pack your crust firmly. Place a second pie pan on top of your crust and apply pressure for added consistency.

- Pie crusts crumble when fats and sugars fail to create a sturdy bond. Mix your ingredients well. Cooling and heating both strengthen the bond.

- Bring your crusts to the edge. Let them overflow. You can remove excess crumbs from the edge of the pie pan with the back of a knife or straight edge to create uniformity.

- Cover your crusts before refrigerating or freezing. They will absorb other odors that altar the taste.

- If the recipe calls for melted butter, cut the butter into ½ inch sections and microwave for 20 seconds at a time.

Pastry Crust Tips & Tricks

- Resist premade frozen crusts. There is no reason to be intimidated by pastry crusts.

- Refrigerate all of your ingredients first, even the flour and salt.

- Use a mixture of cake flour and all-purpose flour for the best crust. Too much cake flour will make the crust delicate. Too much all purpose flour will make it tough.

- Always combine dry ingredients first.

- Butter should be quite cold. If it starts to soften, chill it before continuing.

- For a flakier pie, substitute half of the butter for shortening.

- Mix until dry ingredients combine with butter to form very small pea shapes before adding water.

- Pockets of fat create flakey layers. Use two knives to cut butter into the pastry and allow some of the pea sized portions to remain.

- The addition of ice water should bind the peas into a single pastry ball.

- Substitute sour cream for water to create a flakier crust.

- Substitute egg for water to create a well-bound, durable crust.

- When rolling dough, lift periodically to prevent sticking. Flour dust your rolling surface and rolling pin.

- Roll dough around rolling pin to transfer to the pie pan without damaging it.

- Brush your crust with egg whites and refrigerate for 20 minutes before baking to add extra protection from a soggy crust.

- Spice up your pastry crust with some of the items on the secret ingredient page. Cinnamon, nutmeg, and most dry spices work well. So do crushed nuts, cookies and cereals.

Traditional Graham Cracker Crust

- Easy to make.
- Lightly sweetened graham flavor.
- A Keys classic.
- Serves: 8

Ingredients

1 ½ cups graham cracker crumbs
1/3 cup white sugar
6 tablespoons butter, melted

Directions

1. Combine crumbs and sugar in a medium bowl.
2. Stir in butter until crumbs are evenly coated.
3. Press and form evenly into a 9-inch pie pan.
4. Refrigerate at least 30 minutes before filling.

Nutrition Facts	
Serving Size 35 g	
Amount Per Serving	
Calories 174	Calories from Fat 91
	% Daily Value*
Total Fat 10.1g	16%
Saturated Fat 5.6g	28%
Cholesterol 23mg	8%
Sodium 96mg	4%
Total Carbohydrates 20.4g	7%
Sugars 13.2g	
Protein 1.2g	
Vitamin A 5%	Vitamin C 0%
Calcium 1%	Iron 3%
Nutrition Grade D+	
* Based on a 2000 calorie diet	

In 1965, Florida State Representative Bernie Papy, Jr. introduced legislation calling for a $100 fine to be levied against anyone advertising Key lime pie that is not made with Key limes. The bill did not pass.

Classic Pastry Crust

- Easy to make.
- Serves: 8

Ingredients

1 ¼ cups all purpose flour
1 tablespoon white sugar
1/8 teaspoon salt
8 tablespoons unsalted butter, chilled
3 tablespoons ice water

Nutrition Facts

Serving Size 41 g

Amount Per Serving

Calories 179	Calories from Fat 105

	% Daily Value*
Total Fat 11.7g	**18%**
Saturated Fat 7.3g	**37%**
Cholesterol 31mg	**10%**
Sodium 117mg	**5%**
Total Carbohydrates 16.5g	**5%**
Dietary Fiber 0.5g	**2%**
Sugars 1.6g	
Protein 2.1g	

Vitamin A 7%	•	Vitamin C 0%
Calcium 1%	•	Iron 5%

Nutrition Grade C-

* Based on a 2000 calorie diet

Directions

1. Combine flour, sugar and salt in a medium bowl.
2. Divide butter into 8 slices. Work into dry ingredients with fingers until pea sized balls form.
3. Add ice water and mix with fork. Form into flat disk, wrap in plastic and refrigerate 45 minutes.
4. Preheat oven to 425°F
5. Roll dough to 12" diameter and lay in 9" pie pan. Trim edges.
6. Bake at 425°F for 15-20 minutes. Let cool before filling.

As of July 1, 2006, Key lime pie is the Florida State Pie.

Duval Street Double Crust

- Thick crust.
- Extra graham flavor & texture.
- Adds substance if you skip toppings.
- Serves: 8

Ingredients

2 cups graham cracker crumbs
½ cup white sugar
8 tablespoons butter, melted

Nutrition Facts		
Serving Size 51 g		
Amount Per Serving		
Calories 244		Calories from Fat 122
		% Daily Value*
Total Fat 13.5g		**21%**
Saturated Fat 7.3g		**36%**
Trans Fat 0.0g		
Cholesterol 31mg		**10%**
Sodium 268mg		**11%**
Total Carbohydrates 29.8g		**10%**
Dietary Fiber 1.3g		**5%**
Sugars 16.5g		
Protein 1.5g		
Vitamin A 7%	•	Vitamin C 0%
Calcium 0%	•	Iron 5%
Nutrition Grade F		
* Based on a 2000 calorie diet		

Directions

1. Combine crumbs and sugar in a medium bowl.
2. Stir in butter until crumbs are evenly coated.
3. Press and form evenly into a 9-inch pie pan.
4. Refrigerate at least 30 minutes before filling.

9% of Americans prefer to eat their pie crust-first.

S'more To Adore Crust

- Great campfire s'more taste.
- No flaming marshmallows on a burnt stick.
- Serves: 8

Nutrition Facts		
Serving Size 68 g		
Amount Per Serving		
Calories 290		Calories from Fat 119
		% Daily Value*
Total Fat 13.2g		**20%**
Saturated Fat 7.4g		**37%**
Trans Fat 0.0g		
Cholesterol 31mg		**10%**
Sodium 244mg		**10%**
Total Carbohydrates 42.1g		**14%**
Dietary Fiber 1.5g		**6%**
Sugars 22.4g		
Protein 1.6g		
Vitamin A 7%	•	Vitamin C 0%
Calcium 0%	•	Iron 9%
Nutrition Grade D		
* Based on a 2000 calorie diet		

Ingredients

1 ½ cups graham cracker crumbs
¼ cup white sugar
2 tablespoons unsweetened baking cocoa
8 tablespoons butter, melted
1 cup mini marshmallows

Directions

1. Preheat oven to 375° F.
2. Combine crumbs, sugar and cocoa in a medium bowl.
3. Stir in butter until crumbs are evenly coated.
4. Press and form evenly into a 9-inch pie pan.
5. Top with single layer of marshmallows.
6. Bake at 375° F for 10-12 minutes. Cool before adding your favorite filling.

The first traditional s'more recipe appeared in 1927's "Tramping And Trailing With The Girl Scouts".

The Cereal Killer Crust

- Hints of nuts & honey.
- Added crunch.
- Secret ingredient that will keep them guessing.
- Serves: 8

Ingredients

¾ cup graham cracker crumbs
¾ cup Honey Nut Cheerios® cereal, crushed
1/3 cup white sugar
6 tablespoons butter, melted

Directions

1. Preheat oven to 350° F.
2. Combine crumbs, cereal and sugar in a medium bowl.
2. Stir in butter until crumbs are evenly coated.
3. Press and form evenly into a 9-inch pie pan.
4. Bake at 350° F for 5-8 minutes. Cool before adding your favorite filling.

Nutrition Facts		
Serving Size 32 g		
Amount Per Serving		
Calories 157	Calories from Fat 86	
		% Daily Value*
Total Fat 9.6g		**15%**
Saturated Fat 5.5g		**27%**
Trans Fat 0.0g		
Cholesterol 23mg		**8%**
Sodium 155mg		**6%**
Total Carbohydrates 17.6g		**6%**
Dietary Fiber 0.8g		**3%**
Sugars 11.0g		
Protein 1.0g		
Vitamin A 7%	*	Vitamin C 1%
Calcium 2%		Iron 5%
Nutrition Grade D+		
* Based on a 2000 calorie diet		

"A crust eaten in peace is better than a banquet taken in anxiety."

— Aesop

Cocoa loco Crust

- Smooth chocolate and cocoa undertones.
- Simple cereal crust.
- Serves: 8

Ingredients

¾ cup graham cracker crumbs
¾ cup Cocoa Pebbles® cereal, crushed
1/3 cup white sugar
6 tablespoons butter, melted

Directions

1. Preheat oven to 350° F.
2. Combine crumbs, cereal and sugar in a medium bowl.
2. Stir in butter until crumbs are evenly coated.
3. Press and form evenly into a 9-inch pie pan.
4. Bake at 350° F for 5-8 minutes. Cool before adding your favorite filling.

Nutrition Facts	
Serving Size 32 g	
Amount Per Serving	
Calories 158	Calories from Fat 86
	% Daily Value*
Total Fat 9.5g	**15%**
Saturated Fat 5.6g	**28%**
Trans Fat 0.0g	
Cholesterol 23mg	**8%**
Sodium 151mg	**6%**
Total Carbohydrates 18.0g	**6%**
Dietary Fiber 0.6g	**2%**
Sugars 11.4g	
Protein 0.7g	
Vitamin A 7% •	Vitamin C 0%
Calcium 0% •	Iron 3%
Nutrition Grade D+	
* Based on a 2000 calorie diet	

 The Key Lime is a natural deodorizer. Boil your leftover peels to remove food smells from the kitchen.

Cinnamon Sin Crust

- Unmistakable cinnamon taste.
- Distinct, pleasant aroma.
- Serves: 8

Ingredients

1 ½ cups graham cracker crumbs
1/3 cup white sugar
1 teaspoon ground cinnamon
6 tablespoons butter, melted

Directions

1. Preheat oven to 350° F.
2. Combine crumbs, sugar and cinnamon in a medium bowl.
2. Stir in butter until crumbs are evenly coated.
3. Press and form evenly into a 9-inch pie pan.
4. Bake at 350° F for 5-8 minutes. Cool before adding your favorite filling.

Nutrition Facts	
Serving Size 37 g	
Amount Per Serving	
Calories 179	Calories from Fat 91
	% Daily Value*
Total Fat 10.1g	16%
Saturated Fat 5.5g	27%
Trans Fat 0.0g	
Cholesterol 23mg	8%
Sodium 201mg	8%
Total Carbohydrates 21.6g	7%
Dietary Fiber 1.1g	5%
Sugars 11.3g	
Protein 1.1g	
Vitamin A 5%	Vitamin C 0%
Calcium 1%	Iron 4%
Nutrition Grade F	
* Based on a 2000 calorie diet	

The wealthy English were known for their "Surprise Pies."
Live creatures would pop out when the pie was cut open.

Petronia Street P-B & J Crust

- Kids love it.
- Evokes childhood memories.
- Serves: 8

Ingredients

¾ cup graham cracker crumbs
¾ cup Peanut Butter Cap'n Crunch® cereal
1/3 cup white sugar
1 teaspoon grape Kool-Aid® mix
6 tablespoons butter, melted

Nutrition Facts

Serving Size 32 g

Amount Per Serving

Calories 157	Calories from Fat 87
	% Daily Value*
Total Fat 9.7g	**15%**
Saturated Fat 5.6g	**28%**
Trans Fat 0.0g	
Cholesterol 23mg	**8%**
Sodium 159mg	**7%**
Total Carbohydrates 17.5g	**6%**
Dietary Fiber 0.6g	**3%**
Sugars 11.0g	
Protein 0.8g	

Vitamin A 5%	•	Vitamin C 3%
Calcium 0%	•	Iron 5%

Nutrition Grade F
* Based on a 2000 calorie diet

Directions

1. Preheat oven to 350° F.
2. Combine crumbs, cereal and Kool-Aid® in a medium bowl.
2. Stir in butter until crumbs are evenly coated.
3. Press and form evenly into a 9-inch pie pan.
4. Bake at 350° F for 5-8 minutes. Cool before adding your favorite filling.

The word "comforting" comes to mind
for 47% of Americans when they think of pie.

Cookie Dough Jamboree Crust

- Satisfies the cookie monster in all of us.
- Sweet graham cracker alternative.
- Serves: 8

Ingredients

1 cup flour
½ teaspoon salt
2 tablespoons white sugar
8 tablespoons butter, softened

Nutrition Facts

Nutrition Facts	
Serving Size 33 g	

Amount Per Serving	
Calories 171	Calories from Fat 105

	% Daily Value*
Total Fat 11.7g	**18%**
Saturated Fat 7.3g	**37%**
Cholesterol 31mg	**10%**
Sodium 229mg	**10%**
Total Carbohydrates 15.1g	**5%**
Sugars 3.2g	
Protein 1.7g	

Vitamin A 7%	•	Vitamin C 0%	
Calcium 1%	•	Iron 4%	

Nutrition Grade D-
* Based on a 2000 calorie diet

Directions

1. Combine flour, salt and sugar in a medium bowl.
2. Add butter and work until dough is formed.
3. Press and form evenly into a 9-inch pie pan.
4. Refrigerate at least 30 minutes.
5. Preheat oven to 400° F. Bake for 10-12 minutes.
7. Cool before filling.

"It could be argued that there is an element of entertainment in every pie, as every pie is inherently a surprise by virtue of its crust."
— Janet Clarkson, *Pie: A Global History*

Holiday Snap Crust

- Ginger snap cookie crust.
- Great for holidays.
- Drunk Uncle Larry optional.
- Serves: 8

Ingredients

1 ½ cups finely crushed ginger snaps
¼ cup light brown sugar
6 tablespoons butter, melted

Nutrition Facts

Serving Size 27 g

Amount Per Serving	
Calories 154	Calories from Fat 91

	% Daily Value*
Total Fat 10.1g	**16%**
Saturated Fat 6.2g	**31%**
Trans Fat 0.0g	
Cholesterol 23mg	**8%**
Sodium 138mg	**6%**
Total Carbohydrates 15.0g	**5%**
Sugars 7.4g	
Protein 0.1g	

Vitamin A 5%	•		Vitamin C 0%
Calcium 1%	•		Iron 0%

Nutrition Grade F
* Based on a 2000 calorie diet

Directions

1. Preheat oven to 350° F.
2. Combine snaps and sugar in a medium bowl.
3. Stir in butter until ingredients are evenly coated.
4. Press and form evenly into a 9-inch pie pan.
5. Bake at 350° F for 5-8 minutes. Cool before adding your favorite filling.

A single Key lime seed has the ability to produce two trees.

Oreo® Glory Crust

- Crisp and creamy chocolate flavor.
- Easily recognized crowd pleaser.
- Serves: 8

Ingredients

1 ½ cups Oreo® cookies, crushed
5 tablespoons butter, melted

Directions

1. Place crushed Oreo® cookies in a medium bowl.
2. Stir in butter until Oreo® cookies are evenly coated.
3. Press and form evenly into a 9-inch pie pan.
4. Refrigerate 45 minutes before adding your favorite filling.
5. Save 8 whole Oreo® cookies for garnish.

Nutrition Facts

Serving Size 28 g

Amount Per Serving

Calories 86	Calories from Fat 73

	% Daily Value*
Total Fat 8.1g	13%
Saturated Fat 4.8g	24%
Cholesterol 19mg	6%
Sodium 83mg	3%
Total Carbohydrates 3.2g	1%
Sugars 1.9g	
Protein 0.5g	

Vitamin A 4%	*	Vitamin C 0%
Calcium 0%	*	Iron 1%

Nutrition Grade D-

* Based on a 2000 calorie diet

Rubbing Key lime juice around your sinks and faucets will remove hard water stains and the other kind of lime build up.

Papa's Pretzel Crust

- More twists than a Hemingway novel.
- Perfect for 'sweet and salty' food lovers.
- Nice added crunch.
- Serves: 8

Ingredients

1 ½ cups crushed pretzel sticks
¼ cup light brown sugar
8 tablespoons butter, melted

Nutrition Facts	
Serving Size 36 g	
Amount Per Serving	
Calories 185	Calories from Fat 108
	% Daily Value*
Total Fat 12.0g	18%
Saturated Fat 7.4g	37%
Trans Fat 0.0g	
Cholesterol 31mg	10%
Sodium 321mg	13%
Total Carbohydrates 18.3g	6%
Dietary Fiber 0.5g	2%
Sugars 4.9g	
Protein 1.9g	
Vitamin A 7%	Vitamin C 0%
Calcium 1%	Iron 5%
Nutrition Grade F	
* Based on a 2000 calorie diet	

Directions

1. Preheat oven to 350° F.
2. Combine pretzel crumbs and sugar in a medium bowl.
3. Stir in butter until ingredients are evenly coated.
4. Press and form evenly into a 9-inch pie pan.
5. Bake at 350° F for 8-10 minutes. Cool before adding your favorite filling.

"Visiting the Keys without sampling the Key lime pie
is like being a vegetarian at a Texas BBQ"
— Heather Buchanan

Nutcracker Sweet Crust

- Bursting with pecan flavor.
- Slightly sweet.
- Great nut crunch.
- Serves: 8

Ingredients

1 ½ cup frozen pecans shelled & crushed
¼ cup light brown sugar
5 tablespoons butter, melted

Directions

1. Crush pecans to the size of very small peas.
2. Combine pecans and sugar in a medium bowl.
3. Stir in butter until ingredients are evenly coated.
4. Press and form evenly into a 9-inch pie pan.
5. Refrigerate at least 30 minutes before adding your favorite filling.

Nutrition Facts	
Serving Size 36 g	
Amount Per Serving	
Calories 185	Calories from Fat 108
	% Daily Value*
Total Fat 12.0g	**18%**
Saturated Fat 7.4g	**37%**
Trans Fat 0.0g	
Cholesterol 31mg	**10%**
Sodium 321mg	**13%**
Total Carbohydrates 18.3g	**6%**
Dietary Fiber 0.5g	**2%**
Sugars 4.9g	
Protein 1.9g	
Vitamin A 7%	Vitamin C 0%
Calcium 1%	Iron 5%
Nutrition Grade F	
* Based on a 2000 calorie diet	

1 in 5 Americans have eaten an entire pie by themselves.

Boca Chica Chili Pepper Crust

- Hot and spicy.
- Pleasant after burn.
- Not for sensitive tongues.
- Serves: 8

Ingredients

1 ½ cup graham cracker crumbs
¼ cup white sugar
1 teaspoon crushed red pepper flakes
¼ teaspoon cayenne pepper
6 tablespoons butter, melted

Nutrition Facts		
Serving Size 35 g		
Amount Per Serving		
Calories 171		Calories from Fat 92
		% Daily Value*
Total Fat 10.2g		16%
Saturated Fat 5.5g		27%
Trans Fat 0.0g		
Cholesterol 23mg		8%
Sodium 201mg		8%
Total Carbohydrates 19.4g		6%
Dietary Fiber 1.1g		4%
Sugars 9.3g		
Protein 1.1g		
Vitamin A 8%	•	Vitamin C 0%
Calcium 0%	•	Iron 4%
Nutrition Grade F		
* Based on a 2000 calorie diet		

Directions

1. Combine first three ingredients in a medium bowl.
2. Mix cayenne pepper into melted butter.
3. Stir in butter and blend well until ingredients are evenly coated.
4. Press and form evenly into a 9-inch pie pan.
5. Refrigerate at least 30 minutes before adding your favorite filling.

"Work is the meat of life, pleasure the dessert."

— B.C. Forbes

Thin Mint® Cookie Crust

- Substitute Grasshopper® cookies off-season.
- Wendy Donald's favorite.
- Serves: 8

Ingredients

1 ½ cups Thin Mint® cookies, crushed
4 tablespoons butter, melted

Directions

1. Combine cookies and butter.
2. Press and form evenly into a 9-inch pie pan.
3. Refrigerate at least 30 minutes before filling.
4. Add your favorite filling and bake according to recipe.
5. Save 8 cookies to garnish.

Nutrition Facts		
Serving Size 26 g		
Amount Per Serving		
Calories 63		Calories from Fat 67
		% Daily Value*
Total Fat 7.4g		**11%**
Saturated Fat 4.8g		**24%**
Cholesterol 20mg		**7%**
Sodium 50mg		**2%**
Total Carbohydrates 3.4g		**1%**
Sugars 2.4g		
Protein 0.4g		
Vitamin A 4%	*	Vitamin C 0%
Calcium 1%	*	Iron 0%
Nutrition Grade D-		
* Based on a 2000 calorie diet		

"We must have pie. Stress can not exist in the presence of pie."

— David Mamet

Nilla® Wafer Crust

- Crisp vanilla flavor.
- Takes you back in a childhood time machine.
- Serves: 8

Ingredients

1 3/4 cups Nilla® Wafer crumbs
6 tablespoons butter, melted
1 tablespoon light brown sugar

Directions

1. Preheat oven to 350° F.
2. Combine crushed wafers and sugar in a medium bowl.
3. Stir in butter until ingredients are evenly coated.
4. Press and form evenly into a 9-inch pie pan.
5. Bake at 350° F for 5-8 minutes. Cool before adding your favorite filling.
6. Save 8 wafers to garnish.

Nutrition Facts	
Serving Size 20 g	
Amount Per Serving	
Calories 116	Calories from Fat 91
	% Daily Value*
Total Fat 10.1g	**16%**
Saturated Fat 5.8g	**29%**
Trans Fat 0.0g	
Cholesterol 24mg	**8%**
Sodium 90mg	**4%**
Total Carbohydrates 6.4g	**2%**
Sugars 3.9g	
Protein 0.3g	
Vitamin A 5%	Vitamin C 0%
Calcium 1%	Iron 1%
Nutrition Grade D-	
* Based on a 2000 calorie diet	

"Promises and pie crusts are made to be broken."

— Jonathan Swift

Missed Her Coffee Crust

- Subtle coffee complexities.
- Caffeine boost.
- Tastes like a French cafe.
- Serves: 8

Ingredients

1 ½ cups graham cracker crumbs
1/3 cup white sugar
6 tablespoons butter, melted
¼ teaspoon espresso powder

Nutrition Facts

Nutrition Facts	
Serving Size 42 g	
Amount Per Serving	
Calories 179	Calories from Fat 91
	% Daily Value*
Total Fat 10.1g	16%
Saturated Fat 5.5g	27%
Trans Fat 0.0g	
Cholesterol 23mg	8%
Sodium 201mg	8%
Total Carbohydrates 21.5g	7%
Dietary Fiber 1.0g	4%
Sugars 11.3g	
Protein 1.1g	
Vitamin A 5%	Vitamin C 0%
Calcium 0%	Iron 4%
Nutrition Grade D-	
* Based on a 2000 calorie diet	

Directions

1. Combine crumbs and sugar in a medium bowl.
2. Dissolve espresso powder in melted butter. Stir well.
2. Stir butter into crumb mixture until ingredients are evenly coated.
3. Press and form evenly into a 9-inch pie pan.
4. Refrigerate at least 30 minutes before adding your favorite filling.

18% of men say their wife makes the best homemade pie.

Double Rum Yum Crust

- Dark & light rums.
- Flavorful kick.
- Serves: 8

Nutrition Facts		
Serving Size 51 g		
Amount Per Serving		
Calories 220		Calories from Fat 98
		% Daily Value*
Total Fat 10.9g		**17%**
Saturated Fat 3.4g		**17%**
Trans Fat 0.0g		
Cholesterol 7mg		**2%**
Sodium 42mg		**2%**
Total Carbohydrates 27.1g		**9%**
Dietary Fiber 1.6g		**7%**
Sugars 14.5g		
Protein 1.3g		
Vitamin A 0%	•	Vitamin C 0%
Calcium 1%	•	Iron 3%
Nutrition Grade D-		
* Based on a 2000 calorie diet		

Ingredients

½ cup semisweet chocolate chips
2 tablespoons corn syrup
2 tablespoons light rum
2 tablespoons dark rum
1 1/3 cups vanilla wafers, crushed
¼ cup confectioner's sugar
½ cup chopped pecans

Directions

1. Melt chocolate chips in microwave or double boiler, stirring until smooth.
2. Remove from heat. Stir in corn syrup and rum.
3. Combine wafers, sugar and pecans. Stir into chocolate mixture.
4. Press and form evenly into a 9-inch pie pan.
5. Refrigerate for one hour before adding your favorite filling.

2% of women say their husband makes the best homemade pie.

No Mistakin' Bacon Crust

- Delicious bacon flavor.
- Sweet & smoky.
- Love at first bite.
- Serves: 8

Nutrition Facts	
Serving Size 53 g	
Amount Per Serving	
Calories 269	Calories from Fat 168
	% Daily Value*
Total Fat 18.6g	29%
Saturated Fat 8.9g	44%
Cholesterol 52mg	17%
Sodium 504mg	21%
Total Carbohydrates 15.1g	5%
Sugars 9.1g	
Protein 10.4g	
Vitamin A 5%	Vitamin C 1%
Calcium 1%	Iron 5%
Nutrition Grade F	
* Based on a 2000 calorie diet	

Ingredients

1 ¼ cups graham cracker crumbs
¾ cup apple wood smoked bacon
6 tablespoons butter, melted
¼ cup brown sugar

Directions

1. Render bacon, removing fat from pan frequently. Save fat for a bacon filling.
2. Crisp bacon. Chop fine.
3. Combine bacon, graham crackers and brown sugar in a medium bowl.
4. Stir in melted butter until ingredients are evenly coated.
5. Press into a 9" pie pan. Refrigerate for 30 minutes.

In the 19th Century, fruit pies were a fairly common breakfast item.

Fillings... Nothing More Than Fillings

Filling Tips & Tricks

Eggs:

- Egg yolks bind ingredients and thicken to create a smooth, rich Key lime pie filling. Many recipes separate yolks from whites so the whites can be used for a meringue topping. Egg whites hold air better and add volume. Feel free to experiment with egg whites in your filling if you are not making meringue. Start with one white.

- Use fresh eggs. Eggs age more in one day at room temperature than one week in the refrigerator. A fresh egg will sink in water. An older egg will stand up.

- A cloudy egg white is a sign of freshness, not age; it is caused by a high carbon dioxide content when the egg is laid.

- The egg yolk and white separate best when cold. Egg whites will beat to a better volume if they're allowed to stand at room temperature for 20 to 30 minutes before beating.

- All of the recipes call for large eggs. Other sizes will work for recipes using 3 eggs. If using more, adjust according to the egg size you are using.

- Separate eggs by cracking the shell in half and cradling the yolk back and forth between the two halves as the whites drain to a bowl below. Cracking the whole egg into a bowl, and holding a partially squeezed, empty water bottle directly over the yolk can also remove yolks. Gently release pressure on the bottle to create a suction effect and suck up the yolk for transfer to a new bowl.

Sweetened Condensed Milk:
- Don't confuse sweetened condensed milk with evaporated milk or other canned milk products. This will ruin your pie.

- Condensed milk is nourishing, but high in sugar. Fat free versions provide great taste and are worth trying.

- Sweetened condensed milk provides smoothness and sweetness. Use a spatula to get all of the contents out of the can.

- Ensure eggs and sweetened condensed milk are mixed well before adding Key lime juice.

- Use sweetened condensed milk as a sauce before serving. It's also great with French toast.

Key Lime Juice:
- Fresh Key limes are best, but bottled Key lime juice will do the trick. If neither is available, mix equal parts lemon and Persian lime to create an imposter Key lime juice.

- Get more juice out of your Key limes by washing them with soapy water, rinsing and microwaving for thirty seconds.

- Roll whole Key limes between counter and palm of your hand before juicing.

- Poke the Key lime with a fork to avoid uncontrolled juice spray.

- Annoyed by seeds? Use a garlic press to juice your Key limes.

- The acid in Key limes reacts with aluminum and can affect the flavor. Avoid using aluminum pans or aluminum foil when making a Key lime pie.

- Invest in a zester. They are inexpensive. Zest adds flavors from the citrus oils that enhance the pie. They are great for creating garnish twists too.

- Always add the Key lime juice after eggs and sweetened condensed milk.

- The acidity in Key lime juice causes a reaction with the sweetened condensed milk known as souring, which causes it to thicken on its own. Key lime pies are baked today to avoid the health risks of salmonella in eggs. If you plan on a no bake pie, be sure to use pasteurized eggs.

- Don't worry when your filling does not fill the pie pan. It will increase in size as it thickens and the topping will add volume.

Classic Filling

- A standard Key West recipe.
- Easy to make.
- Classic taste.
- Serves: 8

Ingredients

1 14-ounce can sweetened condensed milk

4 egg yolks

½ cup Key lime juice

Nutrition Facts

Serving Size 125 g

Amount Per Serving

Calories 206	Calories from Fat 59

	% Daily Value*
Total Fat 6.6g	10%
Saturated Fat 3.5g	18%
Cholesterol 122mg	41%
Sodium 67mg	3%
Total Carbohydrates 34.3g	11%
Dietary Fiber 2.0g	8%
Sugars 27.0g	
Protein 5.3g	

Vitamin A 5%		Vitamin C 37%
Calcium 15%		Iron 2%

Nutrition Grade B

* Based on a 2000 calorie diet

Directions

1. Preheat oven to 350° F.
2. Combine sweetened condensed milk and eggs. Mix well.
3. Slowly incorporate Key lime juice.
4. Pour mixture into your favorite prepared crust.
5. Bake at 350° F for 8-10 minutes.
6. Let cool, then chill until firm.
7. Serve with your favorite sauce, topping and garnish.

Condensed milk is wonderful. I don't see how they can get a cow to sit down on those little cans.

—Fred Allen

Best Zest Filling

- Enhanced Key lime flavor.
- Added texture.
- Serves: 8

Ingredients

3 egg yolks
2 teaspoons lime zest
1 14-oz can sweetened condensed milk
½ cup Key lime juice

Nutrition Facts	
Serving Size 123 g	
Amount Per Serving	
Calories 200	Calories from Fat 54
	% Daily Value*
Total Fat 6.0g	**9%**
Saturated Fat 3.3g	**17%**
Cholesterol 96mg	**32%**
Sodium 66mg	**3%**
Total Carbohydrates 34.3g	**11%**
Dietary Fiber 2.0g	**8%**
Sugars 27.0g	
Protein 4.9g	
Vitamin A 4%	Vitamin C 38%
Calcium 15%	Iron 1%
Nutrition Grade B	
* Based on a 2000 calorie diet	

Directions

1. Preheat oven to 350° F.
2. Combine eggs and lime zest. Mix well.
3. Add sweetened condensed milk. Continue mixing.
4. Slowly incorporate Key lime juice.
5. Pour mixture into your favorite prepared crust.
6. Bake at 350° F for 8-10 minutes.
7. Let cool, then chill until firm.
8. Serve with your favorite sauce, topping and garnish.

"Have it jest as you've a mind to, but I've proved it time on time, if you want to change her nature you have got to give her lime."

— Rudyard Kipling

Ice Cream Dream Filling

- Based on Mrs. Butter's classic.
- A favorite of President Truman.
- Serves: 8

Ingredients

6 egg yolks
1 14-oz can sweetened condensed milk
1 cup vanilla bean ice cream, softened
½ cup Key lime juice

Nutrition Facts	
Serving Size 142 g	
Amount Per Serving	
Calories 236	Calories from Fat 77
	% Daily Value*
Total Fat 8.6g	**13%**
Saturated Fat 4.4g	**22%**
Trans Fat 0.0g	
Cholesterol 177mg	**59%**
Sodium 74mg	**3%**
Total Carbohydrates 36.2g	**12%**
Dietary Fiber 2.0g	**8%**
Sugars 28.8g	
Protein 6.3g	
Vitamin A 7%	Vitamin C 37%
Calcium 17%	Iron 2%
Nutrition Grade B	
* Based on a 2000 calorie diet	

Directions

1. Preheat oven to 350° F.
2. Combine sweetened condensed milk and eggs. Mix well.
3. Add ice cream. Mix until smooth.
4 Slowly incorporate Key lime juice.
5. Pour mixture into your favorite prepared crust.
6. Bake at 350° F for 8-10 minutes. Let cool, then freeze.
7. Serve with your favorite sauce, topping and garnish.

More than 1/3 of Americans have eaten pie in bed.

Lower Fat Filing

- Lower fat with rich flavor.
- Light texture.
- Serves: 8

Nutrition Facts

Serving Size 150 g

Amount Per Serving	
Calories 188	Calories from Fat 3

	% Daily Value*
Total Fat 0.3g	0%
Trans Fat 0.0g	
Cholesterol 1mg	0%
Sodium 83mg	3%
Total Carbohydrates 43.5g	15%
Dietary Fiber 2.0g	8%
Sugars 36.0g	
Protein 6.9g	

Vitamin A 4%	•	Vitamin C 35%
Calcium 21%	•	Iron 0%

Nutrition Grade C+
* Based on a 2000 calorie diet

Ingredients

1 14-ounce can nonfat sweetened condensed milk.
2/3 cup low fat Key lime yogurt
½ cup Key lime juice
2 tablespoons water
1 ½ teaspoons unflavored gelatin

Directions

1. Preheat oven to 350° F.
2. Combine sweetened condensed milk and yogurt. Mix well.
3. Slowly incorporate Key lime juice.
4. Stir gelatin into water and microwave for 30 seconds then add to mixture.
5. Bake at 350° F for 8-10 minutes. Let cool, then chill until firm.
6. Serve with your favorite sauce, topping and garnish.

"Cut my pie into four pieces, I don't think I could eat eight."

— Yogi Berra

Two Odd Creams Filling

- Cream cheese and sour cream.
- Sounds odd. Tastes great.
- Serves: 8

Ingredients

8 ounces cream cheese, softened
1 14 ounce can sweetened condensed milk
1/3 cup Key lime juice
1 cup sour cream

Nutrition Facts

Serving Size 111 g

Amount Per Serving	
Calories 320	Calories from Fat 182

	% Daily Value*
Total Fat 20.2g	**31%**
Saturated Fat 12.7g	**64%**
Trans Fat 0.0g	
Cholesterol 61mg	**20%**
Sodium 162mg	**7%**
Total Carbohydrates 29.0g	**10%**
Sugars 27.1g	
Protein 7.0g	

Vitamin A 14%	•		Vitamin C 3%
Calcium 20%	•		Iron 3%

Nutrition Grade C
* Based on a 2000 calorie diet

Directions

1. Mix cream cheese until soft.
2. Add sweetened condensed milk. Mix well.
3. Slowly incorporate Key lime juice.
5. Add sour cream and mix until smooth.
6. Pour into your favorite cooled, prepared crust.
7. Refrigerate for 2 hours before serving.

7% of Americans have passed off a store-bought pie as homemade.

Have an Avocado Filling

- Yep. Avocado.
- Surprising Key lime texture and taste.
- Serves: 8

Ingredients

2 ripe avocados, peeled, pitted
1 14 ounce can sweetened condensed milk
8 ounces cream cheese
½ cup Key lime juice

Nutrition Facts

Serving Size 128 g

Amount Per Serving

Calories 339	Calories from Fat 194

	% Daily Value*
Total Fat 21.6g	33%
Saturated Fat 10.0g	50%
Cholesterol 48mg	16%
Sodium 150mg	6%
Total Carbohydrates 32.0g	11%
Dietary Fiber 3.4g	13%
Sugars 27.4g	
Protein 7.1g	

Vitamin A 12%	•	Vitamin C 11%
Calcium 17%	•	Iron 4%

Nutrition Grade B-
* Based on a 2000 calorie diet

Directions

1. Combine all ingredients and blend well.
2. Pour into your favorite prepared crust.
3. Refrigerate overnight, or at least 6 hours before serving.

Avocados are a fruit, not a vegetable. They are often added to ice cream in Brazil.

Blueberry Bliss Filling

- Great Key lime & blueberry taste.
- Swirls add to flavor and presentation.
- Serves: 8

Ingredients

2 cups blueberries

3 tablespoons water

¼ cup sugar

1 14-ounce can sweetened condensed milk

6 egg yolks

½ cup plus two teaspoons Key Lime juice

Nutrition Facts

Serving Size 177 g

Amount Per Serving

Calories 265 — Calories from Fat 70

% Daily Value*

Total Fat 7.8g	**12%**
Saturated Fat 4.0g	**20%**
Cholesterol 174mg	**58%**
Sodium 70mg	**3%**
Total Carbohydrates 45.9g	**15%**
Dietary Fiber 2.9g	**11%**
Sugars 36.9g	
Protein 6.2g	

Vitamin A 7%	•	Vitamin C 43%
Calcium 16%	•	Iron 3%

Nutrition Grade B

* Based on a 2000 calorie diet

Directions

1. Preheat oven to 350° F.

2. For blueberry compote, combine blueberries, water, sugar and 2 teaspoons of Key lime juice. Cook in saucepan at medium heat for 10 minutes. Set aside.

2. Combine sweetened condensed milk and eggs. Mix well.

3. Slowly incorporate remaining Key lime juice.

4. Pour mixture into your favorite prepared crust.

6. Drizzle with blueberry compote. Cut through mixture with knife to swirl.

5. Bake at 350° F for 8-10 minutes.

6. Let cool, then chill until firm.

Mango Tango Filling

- Great Key lime & mango taste.
- Easy to make.
- Serves: 8

Ingredients

2 cups diced mango
3 tablespoons water
¼ cup sugar
1 14-ounce can sweetened condensed milk
6 egg yolks
½ cup plus two teaspoons Key lime juice

Directions

1. Preheat oven to 350° F.
2. For mango compote, combine mango, water, sugar and 2 teaspoons of Key lime juice. Cook in saucepan at medium heat for 10 minutes. Set aside.
2. Combine sweetened condensed milk and eggs. Mix well.
3. Slowly incorporate remaining Key lime juice.
4. Pour mixture into your favorite prepared crust.
6. Drizzle with mango compote. Cut through mixture with knife to swirl.
5. Bake at 350° F for 8-10 minutes.
6. Let cool, then chill until firm.

Nutrition Facts

Serving Size 182 g

Amount Per Serving

Calories 271 — Calories from Fat 70

% Daily Value*

Total Fat 7.8g	12%
Saturated Fat 4.0g	20%
Cholesterol 174mg	58%
Sodium 70mg	3%
Total Carbohydrates 47.7g	16%
Dietary Fiber 2.7g	11%
Sugars 39.4g	
Protein 6.2g	

Vitamin A 13%	•	Vitamin C 56%
Calcium 16%	•	Iron 3%

Nutrition Grade B

* Based on a 2000 calorie diet

Cappuccino Swirl Filling

- Classic Key lime with a cappuccino kick.
- Serves: 8

Ingredients

20 oz (1.5cans) sweetened condensed milk
6 eggs
½ cup Key lime juice
2 teaspoons cappuccino powder or instant coffee

Nutrition Facts	
Serving Size 172 g	
Amount Per Serving	
Calories 295	Calories from Fat 85
	% Daily Value*
Total Fat 9.4g	15%
Saturated Fat 4.9g	25%
Trans Fat 0.0g	
Cholesterol 147mg	49%
Sodium 136mg	6%
Total Carbohydrates 45.8g	15%
Dietary Fiber 2.0g	8%
Sugars 38.8g	
Protein 9.8g	
Vitamin A 7%	Vitamin C 38%
Calcium 22%	Iron 4%
Nutrition Grade B	
* Based on a 2000 calorie diet	

Directions

1. Preheat oven to 350° F.
2. Combine 14 ounces of condensed milk and eggs. Mix well.
3. Slowly incorporate Key lime juice.
4. Pour mixture into your favorite prepared crust.
5. Stir cappuccino powder into remaining condensed milk and drizzle over pie in a circular motion to create swirls.
6. Bake at 350° F for 8-10 minutes.
6. Let cool, then chill until firm.
7. Serve with your favorite sauce, topping and garnish.

 **6 million men between the ages of 35 and 54 have eaten the last slice of pie and denied it.**

Vaca Key Vanilla Filling

- Great for vanilla freaks.
- Classic flavor with a kick.
- Serves: 8

Ingredients

6 egg yolks
1 14-oz can sweetened condensed milk
1 teaspoon vanilla extract
½ cup Key lime juice

Nutrition Facts

Serving Size 130 g

Amount Per Serving

Calories 221	Calories from Fat 69

	% Daily Value*
Total Fat 7.7g	**12%**
Saturated Fat 3.9g	**20%**
Cholesterol 174mg	**58%**
Sodium 69mg	**3%**
Total Carbohydrates 34.5g	**12%**
Dietary Fiber 2.0g	**8%**
Sugars 27.1g	
Protein 5.9g	

Vitamin A 6%	•	Vitamin C 37%
Calcium 16%	•	Iron 2%

Nutrition Grade C
* Based on a 2000 calorie diet

Directions

1. Preheat oven to 350° F.
2. Combine sweetened condensed milk, eggs and vanilla. Mix well.
3. Slowly incorporate Key lime juice.
4. Pour mixture into your favorite prepared crust.
5. Bake at 350° F for 8-10 minutes.
6. Let cool, then chill until firm.
7. Serve with your favorite sauce, topping and garnish.

To get more juice out of your limes, simply wash them well with soap and water, rinse, and then pop them in the microwave for 30 to 40 seconds on high.

Yummy Rummy Filling

- Rum for an added taste of the islands.
- Drink while preparing for added adventure.
- Serves: 8

Ingredients

6 egg yolks
1 14-oz can sweetened condensed milk
2 ounces coconut rum (white rum is fine)
½ cup Key lime juice

Nutrition Facts	
Serving Size 136 g	
Amount Per Serving	
Calories 236	Calories from Fat 69
	% Daily Value*
Total Fat 7.7g	**12%**
Saturated Fat 3.9g	**20%**
Cholesterol 174mg	**58%**
Sodium 69mg	**3%**
Total Carbohydrates 34.5g	**11%**
Dietary Fiber 2.0g	**8%**
Sugars 27.1g	
Protein 5.9g	
Vitamin A 6%	Vitamin C 37%
Calcium 16%	Iron 2%
Nutrition Grade C	
* Based on a 2000 calorie diet	

Directions

1. Preheat oven to 350° F.
2. Combine sweetened condensed milk and eggs. Mix well.
3. Add rum and continue to mix.
4. Slowly incorporate Key lime juice.
5. Pour mixture into your favorite prepared crust.
6. Bake at 350° F for 8-10 minutes.
7. Let cool, then chill until firm.
8. Serve with your favorite sauce, topping and garnish.

A six string - 10 shots - of Cruzan rum, hey, I like it a lot.
With my, my, my - my Key lime pie.

—Kenny Chesney, *Key Lime Pie*

Chocolate Chip Charm Filling

- Chocolate lovers delight.
- Serves: 8

Ingredients

1 14-ounce can sweetened condensed milk
4 egg yolks
½ cup Key lime juice
¾ cup semi sweet chocolate chips

Nutrition Facts		
Serving Size 131 g		
Amount Per Serving		
Calories 236		Calories from Fat 73
		% Daily Value*
Total Fat 8.1g		**12%**
Saturated Fat 4.3g		**21%**
Cholesterol 122mg		**41%**
Sodium 71mg		**3%**
Total Carbohydrates 38.0g		**13%**
Dietary Fiber 2.4g		**10%**
Sugars 30.4g		
Protein 5.6g		
Vitamin A 5%	•	Vitamin C 37%
Calcium 15%	•	Iron 5%
Nutrition Grade B-		
* Based on a 2000 calorie diet		

Directions

1. Preheat oven to 350° F.
2. Combine sweetened condensed milk and eggs. Mix well.
3. Slowly incorporate Key lime juice.
4. Stir in chocolate chips.
5. Pour mixture into your favorite prepared crust.
6. Bake at 350° F for 8-10 minutes.
7. Let cool, then chill until firm.
8. Serve with your favorite sauce, topping and garnish.

Nearly one in four women believe they make the best pie — better than their mother or grandmother.

Makin' Bacon Filling

- Star of any pot-luck.
- Try with bacon or chili pepper crust.
- Serves: 8

Ingredients

1 14-ounce can sweetened condensed milk

4 egg yolks

3 tablespoons bacon fat

½ cup Key lime juice

Nutrition Facts

Serving Size 132 g

Amount Per Serving

Calories 245	Calories from Fat 86

	% Daily Value*
Total Fat 9.6g	15%
Saturated Fat 4.5g	23%
Trans Fat 0.0g	
Cholesterol 130mg	43%
Sodium 232mg	10%
Total Carbohydrates 34.4g	11%
Dietary Fiber 2.0g	8%
Sugars 27.0g	
Protein 7.9g	

Vitamin A 5%	•	Vitamin C 37%
Calcium 15%		Iron 2%

Nutrition Grade B

* Based on a 2000 calorie diet

Directions

1. Preheat oven to 350° F.
2. Combine sweetened condensed milk, eggs and bacon fat. Mix well.
3. Slowly incorporate Key lime juice.
4. Pour mixture into your favorite prepared crust.
5. Bake at 350° F for 8-10 minutes.
6. Let cool, then chill until firm.
7. Serve with your favorite sauce, topping and garnish.

"This pie goes surprisingly well with Miller High Life."

— Christopher Shultz

Mangrove Mint Filling

- Cool mint flavor.
- Subtle chocolate surprises.
- Serves: 8

Ingredients

6 egg yolks
1 14-oz can sweetened condensed milk
1 cup mint chocolate chip ice cream, softened
½ cup Key Lime juice

Nutrition Facts

Nutrition Facts

Serving Size 147 g

Amount Per Serving

Calories 256	Calories from Fat 87

	% Daily Value*
Total Fat 9.7g	**15%**
Saturated Fat 5.2g	**26%**
Cholesterol 182mg	**61%**
Sodium 84mg	**3%**
Total Carbohydrates 38.7g	**13%**
Dietary Fiber 2.1g	**9%**
Sugars 30.9g	
Protein 6.6g	

Vitamin A 8%	•	Vitamin C 37%
Calcium 18%	•	Iron 3%

Nutrition Grade B
* Based on a 2000 calorie diet

Directions

1. Preheat oven to 350° F.
2. Combine sweetened condensed milk and eggs. Mix well.
3. Add ice cream. Mix until smooth.
4 Slowly incorporate Key lime juice.
5. Pour mixture into your favorite prepared crust.
6. Bake at 350° F for 8-10 minutes. Let cool, then freeze.
7. Serve with your favorite sauce, topping and garnish.

The Romans believed eating mint would increase intelligence and stop a person from losing his temper.

Marshmallow Madness Filling

- Good for kids or marshmallow fans.
- Unique texture. Not for everyone.
- Serves: 8

<table>
<tr><td colspan="2">Nutrition Facts</td></tr>
<tr><td colspan="2">Serving Size 146 g</td></tr>
<tr><td colspan="2">Amount Per Serving</td></tr>
<tr><td>Calories 274</td><td>Calories from Fat 60</td></tr>
<tr><td></td><td>% Daily Value*</td></tr>
<tr><td>Total Fat 6.6g</td><td>10%</td></tr>
<tr><td>Saturated Fat 3.5g</td><td>18%</td></tr>
<tr><td>Cholesterol 122mg</td><td>41%</td></tr>
<tr><td>Sodium 84mg</td><td>3%</td></tr>
<tr><td>Total Carbohydrates 50.9g</td><td>17%</td></tr>
<tr><td>Dietary Fiber 2.0g</td><td>8%</td></tr>
<tr><td>Sugars 36.9g</td><td></td></tr>
<tr><td>Protein 5.4g</td><td></td></tr>
<tr><td>Vitamin A 5%</td><td>Vitamin C 37%</td></tr>
<tr><td>Calcium 15%</td><td>Iron 2%</td></tr>
<tr><td colspan="2">Nutrition Grade B-</td></tr>
<tr><td colspan="2">* Based on a 2000 calorie diet</td></tr>
</table>

Ingredients

1 14-ounce can sweetened condensed milk

4 egg yolks

½ cup Key lime juice

1 cup mini marshmallows

Directions

1. Preheat oven to 350° F.
2. Combine sweetened condensed milk and eggs. Mix well.
3. Slowly incorporate Key lime juice.
4. Distribute marshmallows evenly over your favorite prepared crust.
5. Pour mixture over crust, then bake at 350° F for 8-10 minutes.
6. Let cool, then chill until firm.
7. Serve with your favorite sauce, topping and garnish.

Key limes were once brined and shipped as bar limes.

Nutty Professor Filling

- Simple and delicious.
- Flavor kick compensates for altered color.
- Serves: 8

Ingredients

6 egg yolks
1 14-oz can sweetened condensed milk
¾ cup Nuttella® hazelnut spread
½ cup Key lime juice

Nutrition Facts

Serving Size 153 g

Amount Per Serving

Calories 370	Calories from Fat 144
	% Daily Value*
Total Fat 15.9g	**25%**
Saturated Fat 5.4g	**27%**
Cholesterol 174mg	**58%**
Sodium 80mg	**3%**
Total Carbohydrates 51.7g	**17%**
Dietary Fiber 3.5g	**14%**
Sugars 42.1g	
Protein 7.4g	

Vitamin A 6%	•	Vitamin C 37%
Calcium 19%	•	Iron 9%

Nutrition Grade C+
* Based on a 2000 calorie diet

Directions

1. Preheat oven to 350° F.
2. Combine sweetened condensed milk and eggs. Mix well.
3. Add hazelnut spread. Mix until smooth.
4 Slowly incorporate Key lime juice.
5. Pour mixture into your favorite prepared crust.
6. Bake at 350° F for 8-10 minutes. Let cool, then chill until firm.
7. Serve with your favorite sauce, topping and garnish.

Freeze fresh Key lime juice in ice-cube trays. The cubes will store in a freezer bag for about four months.

Peanut Butter Passion Filling

- Key lime peanut butter perfection.
- A new but familiar flavor combination.
- Serves: 8

Ingredients

6 egg yolks
1 14-oz can sweetened condensed milk
¾ cup creamy peanut butter
½ cup Key lime juice

Nutrition Facts		
Serving Size 154 g		
Amount Per Serving		
Calories 362		Calories from Fat 179
		% Daily Value*
Total Fat 19.9g		31%
Saturated Fat 6.5g		32%
Cholesterol 174mg		58%
Sodium 180mg		8%
Total Carbohydrates 39.2g		13%
Dietary Fiber 3.5g		14%
Sugars 29.3g		
Protein 12.0g		
Vitamin A 6%	*	Vitamin C 37%
Calcium 17%	*	Iron 5%
Nutrition Grade B		
* Based on a 2000 calorie diet		

Directions

1. Preheat oven to 350° F.
2. Combine sweetened condensed milk and eggs. Mix well.
3. Add peanut butter. Mix until smooth.
4 Slowly incorporate Key lime juice.
5. Pour mixture into your favorite prepared crust.
6. Bake at 350° F for 8-10 minutes. Let cool, then chill until firm.
7. Serve with your favorite sauce, topping and garnish.

 If you lined up the number of pies sold at U.S. grocery stores in one year, they would circle the globe and then some.

Coconut Loconut Filling

- A true Caribbean taste.
- Nice coconut texture.
- Serves: 8

Ingredients

6 egg yolks
1 14-oz can sweetened condensed milk
½ cup Key lime juice
¾ cup toasted coconut

Directions

1. Preheat oven to 350° F.
2. Toast coconut on baking sheet until golden brown.
3. Combine sweetened condensed milk and eggs. Mix well.
3. Add toasted coconut. Mix until smooth.
4 Slowly incorporate Key lime juice.
5. Pour mixture into your favorite prepared crust.
6. Bake at 350° F for 8-10 minutes. Let cool, then chill until firm.
7. Serve with your favorite sauce, topping and garnish.

Nutrition Facts

Serving Size 137 g

Amount Per Serving

Calories 246 — Calories from Fat 92

	% Daily Value*
Total Fat 10.2g	**16%**
Saturated Fat 6.2g	**31%**
Cholesterol 174mg	**58%**
Sodium 71mg	**3%**
Total Carbohydrates 35.6g	**12%**
Dietary Fiber 2.7g	**11%**
Sugars 27.5g	
Protein 6.2g	

Vitamin A 6%	•	Vitamin C 38%
Calcium 16%	•	Iron 3%

Nutrition Grade B
* Based on a 2000 calorie diet

"If life gives you limes, make margaritas."

— Jimmy Buffett

Fleming Street Flamer Filling

- Not too hot.
- Jalapeno after burn.
- Serves: 8

Ingredients

5 egg yolks
1 14-ounce can sweetened condensed milk
½ cup Key lime juice
¼ cup pureed, pickled jalapenos

Nutrition Facts

Nutrition Facts		
Serving Size 135 g		
Amount Per Serving		
Calories 215		Calories from Fat 64
		% Daily Value*
Total Fat 7.1g		**11%**
Saturated Fat 3.7g		**19%**
Cholesterol 148mg		**49%**
Sodium 168mg		**7%**
Total Carbohydrates 34.9g		**12%**
Dietary Fiber 2.2g		**9%**
Sugars 27.0g		
Protein 5.6g		
Vitamin A 6%	•	Vitamin C 38%
Calcium 15%	•	Iron 2%
Nutrition Grade B		
* Based on a 2000 calorie diet		

Directions

1. Preheat oven to 350° F.
2. Combine sweetened condensed milk and eggs. Mix well.
3. Remove liquid from jalapenos. Stir jalapenos into mixture.
4 Slowly incorporate Key lime juice.
5. Pour mixture into your favorite prepared crust.
6. Bake at 350° F for 8-10 minutes. Let cool, then chill.
7. Serve with your favorite sauce, topping and garnish.

"If God had intended us to follow recipes he wouldn't have given us grandmothers."

— Linda Henley

Tortuga Tea Filling

- Pleasant green tea flavor.
- Serves: 8

Ingredients

1 14-ounce can sweetened condensed milk
4 egg yolks
3 teaspoons green tea powder
½ cup Key lime juice

Directions

1. Preheat oven to 350° F.
2. Combine sweetened condensed milk and eggs. Mix well.
3. Add green tea powder. Continue mixing.
4. Slowly incorporate Key lime juice.
5. Pour mixture into your favorite prepared crust.
6. Bake at 350° F for 8-10 minutes.
7. Let cool, then chill until firm.
8. Serve with your favorite sauce, topping and garnish.

Nutrition Facts	
Serving Size 126 g	
Amount Per Serving	
Calories 208	Calories from Fat 59
	% Daily Value*
Total Fat 6.6g	10%
Saturated Fat 3.5g	18%
Trans Fat 0.0g	
Cholesterol 122mg	41%
Sodium 67mg	3%
Total Carbohydrates 34.3g	11%
Dietary Fiber 2.3g	9%
Sugars 27.0g	
Protein 5.3g	
Vitamin A 7% • Vitamin C 38%	
Calcium 15% • Iron 3%	
Nutrition Grade B	
* Based on a 2000 calorie diet	

British soldiers were issued a daily ration of limes to prevent scurvy. This led to the nickname "limey."

101

To Bake or Not to Bake?

To bake or not to bake? That is the question. Different recipes call for different baking instructions for the crust, filling and toppings. Most of it boils down to health or personal preference. A little knowledge goes a long way when it comes to the different cooking stages of your pie. The following pages discuss the benefits of different methods and the desired results for each.

A husband admires his wife's pie in the 1955 Mrs. America Contest. State Archives of Florida, Charles Barron Collection.

No Bake Crusts: No bake crusts were popular in the Florida Keys before air conditioning and refrigeration came along because they didn't create additional heat. Crumb based pie crusts are best suited for this method, but the crust is more likely to crumble without the benefit of heating or cooling to bind the ingredients with sugar and butter. Some early recipes used crackers and water. Others used Cuban bread.

Refrigerated Crusts: Refrigeration allows the ingredients of both pastry and crumb crust to bond, particularly those where butter has been melted or softened during the preparation. Refrigerating your crusts for 30 minutes before filling, then baking along with the filling gets great results and reduces the chance of over cooking the crust.

Baked Crusts: Baking is another way to bind the ingredients through heating and cooling. Additional flavors are brought out in many ingredients with heat, and baking a crust before filling creates an extra layer of protection against liquids seeping through. Golden brown is the color to look for with most baked crusts.

Frozen Crusts: Freeze crusts if you are in a hurry, but beware of any pre-existing odors in the freezer that will attach to the crust and altar the flavor. Freezing a crust for too long will change the texture and lend the crust to crumbling.

No Bake Fillings: No bake fillings were popular before Salmonella worked its way from the chicken to the egg. Instances are low, but it is not worth the risk. Key limes react with sweetened condensed milk to naturally thicken the pie through souring. Don't risk a no bake pie unless you use pasteurized eggs, an egg substitute, or an alternative pie with avocado, sour cream or cream cheese.

Refrigerated Fillings: Refrigeration speeds the thickening process, helps ingredients bind and can assist in stabilizing many ingredients. Alternative pies such as those mentioned above require longer refrigeration than custard-based pies. Most custard based pies benefit from a combination of baking and refrigeration.

Baked Fillings: Heating binds ingredients, enhances flavors and texture, helps set the filling and kills bacteria. This is the safest method if the recipe uses unpasteurized eggs. Eggs should be heated to 160° F to kill any Salmonella. Baking at 350° F will do the trick.

Frozen Fillings: Frozen pies are a great treat on a hot day. The freezer also comes in handy if you are in a rush or plan on traveling with your pie. Freeze your pie if you use ice cream as an ingredient. For best results, thaw a frozen pie for about 20 minutes before serving.

No Bake Toppings: No bake topping save time and hold up better over time. Meringue topping must be baked. Cream toppings require no baking.

Refrigerated Toppings: Cream toppings are best served cold. Refrigerate them before and after preparation, keeping them cool until served. Whipped cream is best served fresh, but a properly prepared whipped cream will hold up to a night in the refrigerator.

Baked Toppings: Meringue topping can be browned in the oven or with a hand held torch. Heating the meringue kills any salmonella present in the egg and enhances the sugar flavors.

Frozen Toppings: Whipped cream holds up to freezing better than meringue, but it is not ideal for either. The safest topping to freeze? Ice cream.

Photo: David L. Sloan

Simply Sauces

Sauce Tips & Tricks

- Sauces should accent your Key lime pie, not overpower it. I like to sauce the plate so the crust gets most of the sauce's flavor.

- Sauces can go on top of the pie or on the plate beneath. Painting the plate with your sauce creates great visual effects.

- Contain your sauce in a plastic squeeze bottle for added control and dexterity with presentation.

- Use multiple sauces with contrasting colors for added effect and flavor.

- Think zigzag, circular or polka dot formations. Drag a toothpick through your basic shapes to create hearts and sunbursts.

- Sauce too thin? Thicken fruit sauces with a cornstarch slurry.

- Reducing sauces increases the intensity of flavors. If in doubt, less is better.

- At a loss for sauce? Use sweetened condensed milk straight out of the can.

Crème Anglaise Sauce

- Heavenly custard cream sauce.
- Use low heat to avoid scrambled eggs.
- Sauces 8 servings.

Ingredients

1 cup heavy cream
2 tablespoons vanilla extract
4 egg yolks
1/3 cup sugar

Nutrition Facts		
Serving Size 35 g		
Amount Per Serving		
Calories 120		Calories from Fat 70
		% Daily Value*
Total Fat 7.8g		**12%**
Saturated Fat 4.3g		**21%**
Cholesterol 125mg		**42%**
Sodium 10mg		**0%**
Total Carbohydrates 9.5g		**3%**
Sugars 8.8g		
Protein 1.7g		
Vitamin A 7%	•	Vitamin C 0%
Calcium 2%	•	Iron 1%
Nutrition Grade D-		
* Based on a 2000 calorie diet		

Directions

1. Heat cream and vanilla in medium saucepan over low heat until bubbles form at edge.
2. In a separate bowl, whisk egg yolks and sugar until smooth.
3. Slowly whisk half of hot cream mixture into yolks.
4. Slowly whisk egg mixture into saucepan with cream.
5. Stir with wooden spoon until mixture adheres to spoon.
6. Refrigerate before serving if desired.

"When you die, if you get a choice between going to regular heaven or pie heaven, choose pie heaven. It might be a trick, but if it's not, mmmmmmmm, boy."

—Jack Handy

Magic Mango Sauce

- Sweet mango flavors.
- Easy to make.
- Use fresh, ripe mango for best results.
- Sauces 8 servings.

Ingredients

1 cup pureed mango
1 teaspoon brown sugar
1 teaspoon Key lime juice
1 teaspoon orange juice
2 tablespoons water

Directions

1. Combine all ingredients in a medium saucepan over medium heat.
2. Stir until mixture thickens.
3. Remove from heat.
4. Chill before serving if desired.

Nutrition Facts	
Serving Size 26 g	
Amount Per Serving	
Calories 9	Calories from Fat 0
	% Daily Value*
Total Fat 0.0g	0%
Cholesterol 0mg	0%
Sodium 9mg	0%
Total Carbohydrates 2.4g	1%
Sugars 1.4g	
Protein 0.1g	
Vitamin A 1%	Vitamin C 12%
Calcium 0%	Iron 1%
Nutrition Grade B	
* Based on a 2000 calorie diet	

The first mention of a fruit pie in print is from Robert Green's *Arcadia*, 1590.

Star Fruit Carambola Sauce

- Unique tropical taste.
- Mellow fruit flavors.
- Sauces 8 servings.

Ingredients

1 tablespoon butter

1 cup diced star fruit

2 tablespoons sugar

2 tablespoons orange juice

Directions

1. Melt butter in medium saucepan.
2. Add remaining ingredients and stir until boiling.
3. Reduce heat. Simmer until fruit is soft.
4. Remove from heat.
5. Chill before serving if desired.

Nutrition Facts	
Serving Size 22 g	
Amount Per Serving	
Calories 31	Calories from Fat 13
	% Daily Value*
Total Fat 1.5g	2%
Saturated Fat 0.9g	5%
Cholesterol 4mg	1%
Sodium 11mg	0%
Total Carbohydrates 4.5g	1%
Sugars 4.0g	
Protein 0.2g	
Vitamin A 1% •	Vitamin C 11%
Calcium 0% •	Iron 0%
Nutrition Grade C-	
* Based on a 2000 calorie diet	

Some studies suggest the limonin found in Key limes is beneficial in preventing cancer.

Caribbean Coconut Sauce

- Sweet coconut flavor.
- Slight Caribbean kick.
- Sauces 8 servings.

Ingredients

8 ounces sweetened condensed milk

1 egg yolk

2 tablespoons butter

½ cup shredded coconut flakes

¼ teaspoon vanilla extract

Pinch of cayenne pepper

Nutrition Facts

Nutrition Facts	
Serving Size 39 g	
Amount Per Serving	
Calories 141	Calories from Fat 68
	% Daily Value*
Total Fat 7.6g	12%
Saturated Fat 5.1g	25%
Cholesterol 44mg	15%
Sodium 58mg	2%
Total Carbohydrates 16.3g	5%
Sugars 15.8g	
Protein 2.8g	

Vitamin A 4%	•	Vitamin C 2%
Calcium 8%	•	Iron 1%

Nutrition Grade D+

* Based on a 2000 calorie diet

Directions

1. Combine sweetened condensed milk, egg and butter in a medium saucepan.
2. Cook over medium heat until bubbles form at edge.
3. Stir in remaining ingredients and simmer for 2 minutes.
4. Remove from heat. Chill before serving if desired.

Key lime juice prevents oxidation. Sprinkle it on fresh cut fruit to prevent the fruit from browning.

Simple Chocolate Sauce

- Chocolate sauce made easy.
- Simple and rich.
- Sauces 8 servings.

Ingredients

2/3 cup unsweetened cocoa

1 2/3 cups sugar

1 cup milk

1 teaspoon vanilla extract

1 tablespoon corn syrup (to thicken if desired)

Directions

1. Combine cocoa, sugar and milk in a medium saucepan.
2. Bring to a boil over medium heat. Stir while boiling for 1 minute.
3. Remove from heat. Stir in vanilla.
4. Add corn syrup to thicken if necessary.
5. Chill before serving if desired.

Nutrition Facts

Serving Size 82 g

Amount Per Serving

Calories 201	Calories from Fat 14
	% Daily Value*
Total Fat 1.6g	2%
Saturated Fat 1.0g	5%
Cholesterol 2mg	1%
Sodium 14mg	1%
Total Carbohydrates 48.9g	16%
Dietary Fiber 2.4g	10%
Sugars 44.0g	
Protein 2.4g	

Vitamin A 1%	•	Vitamin C 0%
Calcium 5%	•	Iron 6%

Nutrition Grade C-

* Based on a 2000 calorie diet

Key lime juice is an excellent salt alternative.

Cuban Coffee Sauce

- A taste of Cuba.
- Rich coffee flavor.
- Sauces 8 servings.

Ingredients

½ cup heavy cream

½ cup brewed Cuban coffee or espresso

2 egg yolks

½ cup sugar

½ teaspoon vanilla extract

Nutrition Facts	
Serving Size 40 g	
Amount Per Serving	
Calories 89	Calories from Fat 35
	% Daily Value*
Total Fat 3.9g	**6%**
Saturated Fat 2.1g	**11%**
Trans Fat 0.0g	
Cholesterol 63mg	**21%**
Sodium 7mg	**0%**
Total Carbohydrates 12.9g	**4%**
Sugars 12.5g	
Protein 0.8g	
Vitamin A 3% •	Vitamin C 0%
Calcium 1% •	Iron 1%
Nutrition Grade D-	
* Based on a 2000 calorie diet	

Directions

1. Combine heavy cream and coffee in a medium saucepan.
2. Bring to a boil over medium heat.
3. Beat egg yolks with sugar until mixture is thick.
4. Return to saucepan over low heat until mixture thickens.
5. Remove from heat. Stir in vanilla.
6. Chill well before serving.

Oliver Cromwell banned the eating of pie in 1644, declaring it a pagan form of pleasure.

Rum Runner Sauce

- Sweet rum flavor.
- Subtle spice.
- Sauces 8 servings.

Ingredients

2 tablespoons butter
1 tablespoon corn starch
½ cup sugar
1 cup milk
3 tablespoons light rum
Pinch of cardamom

Nutrition Facts

Nutrition Facts

Serving Size 53 g

Amount Per Serving	
Calories 106	Calories from Fat 31

	% Daily Value*
Total Fat 3.5g	5%
Saturated Fat 2.2g	11%
Cholesterol 10mg	3%
Sodium 33mg	1%
Total Carbohydrates 15.1g	5%
Sugars 14.0g	
Protein 1.0g	

Vitamin A 3%	•	Vitamin C 0%
Calcium 4%	•	Iron 0%

Nutrition Grade F

* Based on a 2000 calorie diet

Directions

1. Melt butter in a medium saucepan over medium heat.
2. Combine sugar and cornstarch. Stir into butter.
3. Add milk and stir until boiling.
4. Continue stirring until thick.
5. Remove from heat. Stir in rum and cardamom.
5. Chill before serving if desired.

For 16 years, pie making and eating went underground until the Restoration leaders lifted the ban on pie in 1660.

Key Lime Honey Sauce

- Quick and simple
- Light and flavorful.
- Sauces 8 servings.

Ingredients

1 cup plain yogurt
¼ cup honey
1 tablespoon Key lime juice

Directions

1. Combine yogurt, honey and Key lime juice in a small bowl.
2. Whisk until smooth.
3. Chill before serving.

Nutrition Facts

Serving Size 50 g

Amount Per Serving

Calories 57	Calories from Fat 4

	% Daily Value*
Total Fat 0.4g	**1%**
Cholesterol 2mg	**1%**
Sodium 22mg	**1%**
Total Carbohydrates 11.8g	**4%**
Sugars 11.0g	
Protein 1.8g	

Vitamin A 0%	•	Vitamin C 5%
Calcium 6%	•	Iron 1%

Nutrition Grade A-

* Based on a 2000 calorie diet

"When life gives you limes, rearrange the letters until it spells smile."

— Sofie Christie

Mellow Mint Sauce

- Simple and refreshing.
- Pleasant mint taste.
- Sauces 8 servings.

Ingredients

1 cup plain yogurt
¼ cup finely chopped mint
1 tablespoon Key lime juice
1 tablespoon honey

Directions

1. Combine all ingredients in a small bowl.
2. Whisk until smooth.
3. Chill before serving.

Nutrition Facts		
Serving Size 44 g		
Amount Per Serving		
Calories 34		Calories from Fat 4
		% Daily Value*
Total Fat 0.4g		**1%**
Cholesterol 2mg		**1%**
Sodium 23mg		**1%**
Total Carbohydrates 5.5g		**2%**
Sugars 4.5g		
Protein 1.9g		
Vitamin A 3%	•	Vitamin C 5%
Calcium 6%	•	Iron 2%
Nutrition Grade A		
* Based on a 2000 calorie diet		

Key limes are more susceptible to frost than other citrus fruits.

Begging For Bacon Syrup Sauce

- Lower in fat.
- Nice flavors.
- Excellent healthy alternative.
- Sauces 8 servings.

Ingredients

¼ pound bacon, diced
1 cup maple syrup
8 tablespoons butter
¼ teaspoon ground cinnamon

Directions

1. Render bacon until crispy in a medium saucepan.
2. Add maple syrup and cook over medium heat until it starts to bubble.
3. Remove from heat. Stir in butter and cinnamon.
4. Chill before serving if desired.

Nutrition Facts	
Serving Size 33 g	
Amount Per Serving	
Calories 104	Calories from Fat 11
	% Daily Value*
Total Fat 1.2g	2%
Cholesterol 0mg	0%
Sodium 148mg	6%
Total Carbohydrates 22.2g	7%
Sugars 8.7g	
Protein 1.9g	
Vitamin A 0% •	Vitamin C 0%
Calcium 2% •	Iron 0%
Nutrition Grade D+	
* Based on a 2000 calorie diet	

113 million Americans have eaten pie for breakfast.

Honey Jalapeno Sauce

- Sweet & hot!
- Heat that sneaks.
- Sauces 8 servings.

Ingredients

1 tablespoon butter
2 tablespoons fresh jalapeno, chopped fine
1 cup honey

Nutrition Facts		
Serving Size 46 g		
Amount Per Serving		
Calories 142		Calories from Fat 13
		% Daily Value*
Total Fat 1.4g		**2%**
Saturated Fat 0.9g		**5%**
Cholesterol 4mg		**1%**
Sodium 12mg		**0%**
Total Carbohydrates 35.0g		**12%**
Sugars 34.8g		
Protein 0.2g		
Vitamin A 1%	•	Vitamin C 1%
Calcium 0%	•	Iron 1%
Nutrition Grade D+		
* Based on a 2000 calorie diet		

Directions

1. Melt butter in a medium saucepan over medium heat.
2. Add fresh jalapeno. Cook over medium heat for 1 minute.
3. Add honey and stir. Heat until bubbles form.
5. Remove from heat.
5. Chill before serving if desired.

Key limes are more acidic than Persian or Tahitian limes.

Maple Butter Sauce

- Super Simple.
- Nice flavors.
- Sauces 8 servings.

Ingredients

8 tablespoons butter
4 tablespoons maple syrup
2 tablespoons light brown sugar
Pinch of cinnamon

Directions

1. Combine butter and syrup in a medium saucepan.
2. Cook over medium-low heat until butter melts.
3. Add brown sugar. Stir until melted.
4. Chill before serving if desired.

Nutrition Facts

Serving Size 26 g

Amount Per Serving

Calories 137	Calories from Fat 104

	% Daily Value*
Total Fat 11.5g	18%
Saturated Fat 7.3g	36%
Trans Fat 0.0g	
Cholesterol 31mg	10%
Sodium 83mg	3%
Total Carbohydrates 9.0g	3%
Sugars 8.1g	
Protein 0.1g	

Vitamin A 7%	•	Vitamin C 0%
Calcium 1%	•	Iron 1%

Nutrition Grade D+

* Based on a 2000 calorie diet

"As for butter versus margarine, I trust cows more than chemists."

— Joan Gussow

Key lime Hollandaise Sauce

- Lower in fat.
- Nice flavors.
- Excellent healthy alternative.
- Sauces 8 servings.

Ingredients

4 tablespoons butter
4 egg yolks
1 tablespoon water
2 tablespoons Key lime juice
2 tablespoons light brown sugar
Pinch of salt

Directions

1. Melt butter in medium saucepan then set aside to settle.
2. Whisk egg yolks and water in a double boiler over simmering water until they thicken.
3. When mixture is thick, whisk in butter
4. Whisk in Key lime juice and salt. Serve.

 In Spanish, the Key lime is called lima á cida or lima chica.

Nutrition Facts		
Serving Size 158 g		
Amount Per Serving		
Calories 691	Calories from Fat 577	
		% Daily Value*
Total Fat 64.1g		99%
Saturated Fat 35.7g		178%
Cholesterol 961mg		320%
Sodium 520mg		22%
Total Carbohydrates 20.1g		7%
Sugars 17.9g		
Protein 11.3g		
Vitamin A 48%	*	Vitamin C 0%
Calcium 12%	*	Iron 11%
Nutrition Grade C		
* Based on a 2000 calorie diet		

Whiskey Butter Sauce

- Sweet whiskey flavor.
- Great with holiday Key lime pies.
- Sauces 8 servings.

Ingredients

½ cup whiskey
8 tablespoons butter
¼ cup brown sugar

Nutrition Facts

Nutrition Facts		
Serving Size 33 g		
Amount Per Serving		
Calories 154	Calories from Fat 104	
		% Daily Value*
Total Fat 11.5g		18%
Saturated Fat 7.3g		36%
Cholesterol 31mg		10%
Sodium 83mg		3%
Total Carbohydrates 4.5g		1%
Sugars 4.4g		
Protein 0.1g		
Vitamin A 7%	•	Vitamin C 0%
Calcium 1%	•	Iron 0%
Nutrition Grade F		
* Based on a 2000 calorie diet		

Directions

1. Combine whiskey and 4 tablespoons of butter in a medium saucepan.
2. Cook over medium-low heat, stirring until butter melts.
3. Add brown sugar. Stir until melted.
4. Add remaining butter and stir until mixture thickens.
5. Refrigerate before serving if desired.

In India the Key lime is called kagzi, nimbu, limbu or nebu.

Raspberry Rave Sauce

- Great berry taste.
- Easy to make.
- Sauces 8 servings.

Ingredients

2 cups fresh raspberries
1/3 cup white sugar
2 tablespoons orange juice
2 tablespoons cornstarch
½ cup water

Nutrition Facts

Serving Size 60 g

Amount Per Serving	
Calories 58	Calories from Fat 2

	% Daily Value*
Total Fat 0.2g	0%
Cholesterol 0mg	0%
Sodium 1mg	0%
Total Carbohydrates 14.2g	5%
Dietary Fiber 2.0g	8%
Sugars 10.0g	
Protein 0.4g	

Vitamin A 0%	•	Vitamin C 17%
Calcium 1%	•	Iron 1%

Nutrition Grade A

* Based on a 2000 calorie diet

Directions

1. Combine raspberries, sugar and orange juice in a medium saucepan.
2. Cook over medium heat.
3. Mix cornstarch into water until smooth. Add to saucepan. Bring to boil.
4. Simmer for several minutes while stirring until mixture thickens.
5. Remove from heat. Chill before serving if desired.
6. For a smoother sauce, blend and strain mixture before chilling.

Enhance a glass of water by squeezing in the juice of a single Key lime.

Caramel Kick Sauce

- Great caramel flavor.
- Rich and sticky.
- Sauces 8 servings.

Ingredients

1 cup brown sugar
½ cup heavy cream
4 tablespoons salted butter
1 teaspoon vanilla extract

Nutrition Facts

Serving Size 33 g	

Amount Per Serving	
Calories 147	Calories from Fat 77

	% Daily Value*
Total Fat 8.5g	**13%**
Saturated Fat 5.4g	**27%**
Cholesterol 26mg	**9%**
Sodium 49mg	**2%**
Total Carbohydrates 18.1g	**6%**
Sugars 17.7g	
Protein 0.2g	

Vitamin A 6%	•	Vitamin C 0%
Calcium 2%	•	Iron 1%

Nutrition Grade F
* Based on a 2000 calorie diet

Directions

1. Combine brown sugar, cream and butter in a medium saucepan.
2. Cook over medium-low heat, whisking until mixture thickens.
3. Remove from heat. Stir in vanilla.
4. Chill before serving.

"Seize the moment. Remember all of those women on the Titanic who waved off the dessert cart."

— Erma Bombeck

Blueberry Dream Sauce

- Sweet blueberry flavor.
- Subtle hint of Key lime.
- Sauces 8 servings.

Ingredients

2 cups fresh blueberries
3/4 cup white sugar
½ cup water
1 teaspoon Key lime zest

Nutrition Facts		
Serving Size 70 g		
Amount Per Serving		
Calories 93		Calories from Fat 1
		% Daily Value*
Total Fat 0.1g		**0%**
Cholesterol 0mg		**0%**
Sodium 1mg		**0%**
Total Carbohydrates 24.0g		**8%**
Dietary Fiber 0.9g		**3%**
Sugars 22.3g		
Protein 0.3g		
Vitamin A 0%	•	Vitamin C 6%
Calcium 0%	•	Iron 1%
Nutrition Grade B+		
* Based on a 2000 calorie diet		

Directions

1. Combine blueberries, sugar and water in a medium saucepan.
2. Cook over medium heat, stirring regularly. Bring to a boil.
3. Simmer for several minutes while stirring until mixture thickens.
5. Remove from heat. Stir in Key lime zest.
6. Chill before serving if desired.

3 out of 4 Americans prefer homemade pie, while 13 % enjoy pie from a bakery or pastry shop.

Peanut Butter Fudge Sauce

- Rich chocolate.
- Smooth peanut butter.
- Sauces 8 servings.

Ingredients

½ cup light corn syrup
½ cup creamy peanut butter
¼ cup heavy cream
½ cup semi-sweet chocolate chips

Directions

1. Combine corn syrup, peanut butter and cream in a medium saucepan.
2. Cook over medium heat, stirring regularly. Bring to a boil.
3. Stir in chocolate chips.
4. Simmer for several minutes while stirring until mixture thickens.
5. Remove from heat.
6. Chill before serving if desired.

Nutrition Facts	
Serving Size 43 g	
Amount Per Serving	
Calories 180	Calories from Fat 95
	% Daily Value*
Total Fat 10.5g	16%
Saturated Fat 3.2g	16%
Trans Fat 0.0g	
Cholesterol 5mg	2%
Sodium 76mg	3%
Total Carbohydrates 20.2g	7%
Dietary Fiber 1.2g	5%
Sugars 8.6g	
Protein 4.1g	
Vitamin A 1%	Vitamin C 0%
Calcium 1%	Iron 2%
Nutrition Grade C	
* Based on a 2000 calorie diet	

Lemons float in water. Key limes sink.

Cinnamon Sugar Sauce

- Sweet and simple
- Great cinnamon taste.
- Sauces 8 servings.

Ingredients

1 cup plain yogurt
2 teaspoons light brown sugar
¼ teaspoon ground cinnamon

Directions

1. Combine all ingredients in a small bowl.
2. Whisk until smooth.
3. Chill before serving.

Nutrition Facts

Serving Size 31 g

Amount Per Serving	
Calories 25	Calories from Fat 3

	% Daily Value*
Total Fat 0.4g	**1%**
Trans Fat 0.0g	
Cholesterol 2mg	**1%**
Sodium 22mg	**1%**
Total Carbohydrates 3.0g	**1%**
Sugars 2.9g	
Protein 1.7g	

Vitamin A 0%	•	Vitamin C 0%
Calcium 6%	•	Iron 0%

Nutrition Grade B+

* Based on a 2000 calorie diet

Key limes contain no fat or cholesterol.

Sweet Habanero Sauce

- Sweet tongue fire.
- Best for Key lime daredevils.
- Sauces 8 servings.

Ingredients

2 tablespoons butter

1 habanero pepper, seeds removed, chopped fine

1 14 oz can sweetened condensed milk

Nutrition Facts

Nutrition Facts	
Serving Size 59 g	
Amount Per Serving	
Calories 187	Calories from Fat 65
	% Daily Value*
Total Fat 7.2g	**11%**
Saturated Fat 4.5g	**23%**
Cholesterol 25mg	**8%**
Sodium 84mg	**3%**
Total Carbohydrates 27.5g	**9%**
Sugars 27.3g	
Protein 4.1g	
Vitamin A 5%	Vitamin C 16%
Calcium 14%	Iron 1%
Nutrition Grade B-	
* Based on a 2000 calorie diet	

Directions

1. Melt butter in a medium saucepan over medium heat.
2. Add chopped habanero. Sautee for 1 minute.
3. Stir in sweetened condensed milk. Bring to a boil.
4. Remove from heat.
5. Chill well before serving.

Pie was first introduced to the holiday table at the pilgrim's second Thanksgiving in 1623.

129

No Stopping the Toppings

Whipped Cream Tips & Tricks

- Avoid store bought whipped cream. It liquefies rapidly and does not compare to the real thing in taste or texture.

- Recipes can be prepared with a wire whisk and mixing bowl, but an electric mixer is your friend and can whip up a nice cream in 5 minutes or less.

- Put the heavy cream, stainless steel mixing bowl and whisk or beaters in the freezer for about 20 minutes. The cream will whip faster.

- Resist the urge to over whip your cream. Stop once all ingredients are added and stiff peaks have formed. Over mixing will decrease volume.

- Whipped cream can be flavored with many of the items on the secret ingredient list. Add them last and use moderation.

- Whipped cream holds up better under refrigeration than meringue. It can usually be refrigerated for about 3 days.

Meringue Tips & Tricks

While whipped cream toppings are fairly simple, meringue toppings require a bit more skill and practice. Below are some tips and tricks that apply to just about every meringue recipe. Don't fret if your meringue doesn't come out perfect on the first try. Practice makes perfect, and Key lime pie is just as delicious undressed.

- Moisture is meringue's enemy. Be careful when preparing in high humidity or on rainy days.

- What else is cooking? Steam from other items in your kitchen can compromise the meringue and cause it to weep.

- Eggs should always be room temperature. A room temperature egg incorporates more air. Take them out of the refrigerator 30 minutes in advance, or let the whites sit for 30 minutes after separating.

- Separate eggs using three bowls, only adding whites to third bowl after you are certain no yolks are present. The fat in yolks is another enemy of meringue.

- Salt stabilizes the meringues before sugar is added. Cream of tartar also works as a stabilizer and helps form stiff peaks. **Use a pinch of either for each egg white with the recipes in this book if you choose to use a stabilizer.**

- Use clean dry equipment. Butter, oil, egg yolk and other fats work against the meringue.

- Use a stainless steel or glass bowl, as plastic tends to retain traces of fat.

- Add sugar gradually but don't over mix between sugar additions. Adding sugar too quickly takes air out of the egg whites.

- Undissolved sugar causes beading. A simple way to tell if the sugar is dissolved is to rub a bit of meringue between your thumb and forefinger. If you can feel granules, the sugar is not dissolved enough.

- Meringue is added after the crust and filling have been prepared and baked according to their recipes.

- Spread meringue to edge of the pie to create seal and prevent shrinking.

- Applying meringue to a hot pie allows it to cook from beneath and prevents weeping.

- Working the meringue with a spoon, twisting and twirling can create stiff peaks and swirls.

- To cut a meringue topped pie, dip the knife in water first.

Classic Whipped Cream Topping

- Quick & easy classic.
- Light and tasty.
- Serves: 8

Ingredients

1 cup heavy cream
1 teaspoon vanilla extract
2 tablespoons confectioners' sugar

Nutrition Facts

Serving Size 18 g

Amount Per Serving

Calories 61	Calories from Fat 50

	% Daily Value*
Total Fat 5.5g	9%
Saturated Fat 3.5g	17%
Cholesterol 21mg	7%
Sodium 6mg	0%
Total Carbohydrates 2.4g	1%
Protein 0.3g	

Vitamin A 4%	•	Vitamin C 0%
Calcium 1%	•	Iron 0%

Nutrition Grade F

* Based on a 2000 calorie diet

Directions

1. Chill metal mixing bowl and whisk or beaters in freezer for 10 minutes.
2. Whip cream until stiff peaks are about to form.
3. Add vanilla and sugar.
4. Whip until stiff peaks form. Do not over-mix.
5. Refrigerate until served.

Nearly twice as many people prefer their pie unadorned as those who like it "a la mode" with either ice cream or whipped topping.

Agave Cream Topping

- Lightly sweetened.
- Tasty nectar.
- Serves: 8

Ingredients

1 cup heavy cream
1 teaspoon vanilla extract
2 tablespoons agave nectar

Directions

1. Chill metal mixing bowl and whisk or beaters in freezer for 10 minutes.
2. Whip cream until stiff peaks are about to form.
3. Add vanilla and agave nectar.
4. Whip until stiff peaks form. Do not over-mix.
5. Refrigerate until served.

Nutrition Facts

Serving Size 21 g

Amount Per Serving

Calories 68	Calories from Fat 50

	% Daily Value*
Total Fat 5.5g	9%
Saturated Fat 3.5g	17%
Cholesterol 21mg	7%
Sodium 6mg	0%
Total Carbohydrates 4.5g	1%
Sugars 4.1g	
Protein 0.3g	

Vitamin A 4%	•	Vitamin C 0%
Calcium 1%	•	Iron 0%

Nutrition Grade F
* Based on a 2000 calorie diet

Short's Brewing Company produces a Key lime beer with fresh limes, milk sugar, graham cracker and marshmallow fluff.

Kahlua® Cream Topping

- Coffee liquor flavor.
- A tasty alternative cream.
- Serves: 8

Ingredients

1 cup heavy cream
2 tablespoon confectioners' sugar
1 teaspoon Kahlua® liquor

Directions

1. Chill metal mixing bowl and whisk or beaters in freezer for 10 minutes.
2. Whip cream until stiff peaks are about to form.
3. Add sugar and Kahlua®.
4. Whip until stiff peaks form. Do not over-mix.
5. Chill until served.

Nutrition Facts

Serving Size 21 g

Amount Per Serving

Calories 66	Calories from Fat 50

	% Daily Value*
Total Fat 5.5g	9%
Saturated Fat 3.5g	17%
Cholesterol 21mg	7%
Sodium 6mg	0%
Total Carbohydrates 3.7g	1%
Sugars 1.4g	
Protein 0.3g	

Vitamin A 4%	•	Vitamin C 0%
Calcium 1%	•	Iron 0%

Nutrition Grade F
* Based on a 2000 calorie diet

Several liquors enhance the flavor of whipped cream. Try Baileys®, Grand Marnier®, Frangelico®, or even tequila.

Raspberry Cream Topping

- Great berry taste.
- Light & fresh.
- Serves: 8

Ingredients

¾ cup fresh raspberries
2 teaspoons sugar
1 cup heavy cream

Directions

1. Chill metal mixing bowl and whisk or beaters in freezer.
2. Place raspberries in small bowl and cover with sugar. Let stand for 30 minutes to release juice, then crush with fork.
3. Whip cream until stiff peaks form.
4. Fold raspberry mixture into whipped cream.
5. Chill until served.

Nutrition Facts		
Serving Size 28 g		
Amount Per Serving		
Calories 62		Calories from Fat 51
		% Daily Value*
Total Fat 5.6g		9%
Saturated Fat 3.5g		17%
Cholesterol 21mg		7%
Sodium 6mg		0%
Total Carbohydrates 2.8g		1%
Dietary Fiber 0.8g		3%
Sugars 1.6g		
Protein 0.5g		
Vitamin A 4%	*	Vitamin C 5%
Calcium 1%	*	Iron 0%
Nutrition Grade C		
* Based on a 2000 calorie diet		

Freshen your drain by grinding leftover Key lime skins in the garbage disposal.

Caramel Cream Topping

- Caramel lovers delight.
- Sweet & creamy.
- Serves: 8

Ingredients

1 cup heavy cream
¼ cup brown sugar
1 teaspoon caramel flavor

Directions

1. Chill metal mixing bowl and whisk or beaters in freezer for 10 minutes.
2. Whip cream until stiff peaks are about to form.
3. Add sugar and caramel flavor.
4. Whip until stiff peaks form. Do not over-mix.
5. Chill until served.

Nutrition Facts

Serving Size 20 g

Amount Per Serving	
Calories 70	Calories from Fat 50

	% Daily Value*
Total Fat 5.5g	9%
Saturated Fat 3.5g	17%
Cholesterol 21mg	7%
Sodium 7mg	0%
Total Carbohydrates 4.9g	2%
Sugars 4.5g	
Protein 0.3g	

Vitamin A 4%	•	Vitamin C 0%
Calcium 1%	•	Iron 0%

Nutrition Grade F
* Based on a 2000 calorie diet

Each day in the U.S. there are more than 20 obituaries that mention the deceased's prowess at making pies.

Rum Cream Topping

- Rum. Yum.
- A cream worth raising a toast.
- Serves: 8

Ingredients

1 cup heavy cream
2 tablespoon confectioners' sugar
½ teaspoon vanilla extract
1 teaspoon dark rum

Nutrition Facts

Serving Size 18 g

Amount Per Serving

Calories 61	Calories from Fat 50

	% Daily Value*
Total Fat 5.5g	9%
Saturated Fat 3.5g	17%
Cholesterol 21mg	7%
Sodium 6mg	0%
Total Carbohydrates 2.3g	1%
Protein 0.3g	

Vitamin A 4%	•	Vitamin C 0%
Calcium 1%	•	Iron 0%

Nutrition Grade F

* Based on a 2000 calorie diet

Directions

1. Chill metal mixing bowl and whisk or beaters in freezer for 10 minutes.
2. Whip cream until stiff peaks are about to form.
3. Add sugar, vanilla and rum.
4. Whip until stiff peaks form. Do not over-mix.
5. Chill until served.

At least 15 obituaries in the last three years have claimed the deceased made the best Key lime pie around.

Tabasco® Cream Topping

- Nice and hot.
- Heats and cools.
- Serves: 8

Ingredients

1 cup heavy cream
1 teaspoon Tabasco® sauce

Directions

1. Chill metal mixing bowl and whisk or beaters in freezer for 10 minutes.
2. Whip cream until stiff peaks are about to form.
3. Add Tabasco® sauce.
4. Whip until stiff peaks form. Do not over-mix.
5. Chill until served.

Nutrition Facts

Serving Size 16 g

Amount Per Serving

Calories 52	Calories from Fat 50

	% Daily Value*
Total Fat 5.5g	9%
Saturated Fat 3.5g	17%
Cholesterol 21mg	7%
Sodium 21mg	1%
Total Carbohydrates 0.4g	0%
Protein 0.3g	

Vitamin A 4%	*	Vitamin C 0%
Calcium 1%	*	Iron 0%

Nutrition Grade D

* Based on a 2000 calorie diet

The Armed Forces of The Conch Republic settle disputes by dueling with Key lime pie at 5 paces.

Eggnog Cream Topping

- Holiday spice flavor.
- A Christmas treat.
- Serves: 8

Ingredients

1 cup heavy cream
½ cup eggnog
2 tablespoons confectioners' sugar
¼ teaspoon nutmeg

Nutrition Facts		
Serving Size 33 g		
Amount Per Serving		
Calories 81		Calories from Fat 61
		% Daily Value*
Total Fat 6.8g		10%
Saturated Fat 4.2g		21%
Cholesterol 30mg		10%
Sodium 14mg		1%
Total Carbohydrates 4.5g		1%
Sugars 1.4g		
Protein 0.9g		
Vitamin A 5%	•	Vitamin C 1%
Calcium 3%	•	Iron 0%
Nutrition Grade C-		
* Based on a 2000 calorie diet		

Directions

1. Chill metal mixing bowl and whisk or beaters in freezer for 10 minutes.
2. Whip cream and eggnog until stiff peaks are about to form.
3. Add sugar. Whip until stiff peaks form. Do not over-mix.
4. Fold in nutmeg.
5. Chill until served.

Key Lime Martini: 2 oz. Stoli® Vanil, 1 oz. Liquor 43, 1.5 oz. Cream (half n half), 1 tablespoon of fresh lime juice. Rim with graham cracker crumbs.

Mango Cream Topping

- Creamy mango.
- Light fruit flavor.
- Serves: 8

Ingredients

1 cup pureed mango
2 teaspoons sugar
1 cup heavy cream

Nutrition Facts

Nutrition Facts	
Serving Size 29 g	
Amount Per Serving	
Calories 60	Calories from Fat 50
	% Daily Value*
Total Fat 5.5g	9%
Saturated Fat 3.5g	17%
Cholesterol 21mg	7%
Sodium 14mg	1%
Total Carbohydrates 2.6g	1%
Sugars 2.0g	
Protein 0.3g	
Vitamin A 6%	Vitamin C 8%
Calcium 1%	Iron 0%
Nutrition Grade D+	
* Based on a 2000 calorie diet	

Directions

1. Chill metal mixing bowl and whisk or beaters in freezer.
2. Place mango in small bowl and cover with sugar. Let stand for 30 minutes to release juice, then crush with fork.
3. Whip cream until stiff peaks form.
4. Fold mango mixture into whipped cream.
5. Chill until served.

"You can't imagine what satisfaction can be gotten from throwing a pie into someone's face."
— Emma Thompson

Simple Meringue Topping

- A simple classic.
- Tops 9-inch pie.
- Serves: 8

Ingredients

3 egg whites
6 tablespoons confectioners' sugar, sifted
Pinch of salt per egg white

Nutrition Facts

Serving Size 20 g

Amount Per Serving

Calories 28	Calories from Fat 0

	% Daily Value*
Total Fat 0.0g	0%
Cholesterol 0mg	0%
Sodium 40mg	2%
Total Carbohydrates 5.7g	2%
Protein 1.4g	

Vitamin A 0%	*	Vitamin C 0%	
Calcium 0%	*	Iron 0%	

Nutrition Grade C
* Based on a 2000 calorie diet

Directions

1. Preheat oven to 350° F.
2. Beat egg whites with salt at medium speed until frothy.
3. Add sugar one tablespoon at a time. Continue beating until stiff.
5. Spread meringue over pie.
6. Bake at 350° F. until peaks are golden brown. (10-15 minutes)

Don't tease your egg whites. They can't take a yolk.

Coffee Meringue Topping

- Great coffee taste.
- Tops 9-inch pie.
- Serves: 8

Ingredients

3 egg whites
6 tablespoons confectioners' sugar, sifted
Pinch of salt per egg white
1 teaspoon instant coffee powder

Nutrition Facts		
Serving Size 21 g		
Amount Per Serving		
Calories 28		Calories from Fat 0
		% Daily Value*
Total Fat 0.0g		**0%**
Trans Fat 0.0g		
Cholesterol 0mg		**0%**
Sodium 40mg		**2%**
Total Carbohydrates 5.7g		**2%**
Protein 1.4g		
Vitamin A 0%	•	Vitamin C 0%
Calcium 0%	•	Iron 0%
Nutrition Grade C		
* Based on a 2000 calorie diet		

Directions

1. Preheat oven to 350° F.
2. Beat egg whites and salt at medium speed until frothy.
3. Add sugar one tablespoon at a time. Add coffee and continue beating until stiff.
4. Spread meringue over pie.
5. Bake at 350° F. until peaks are golden brown. (10-15 minutes)

As a hen grows older, she produces larger eggs.

Cinnamon Meringue Topping

- Added cinnamon flavor.
- Tops 9-inch pie.
- Serves: 8

Ingredients

3 egg whites
6 tablespoons confectioners' sugar, sifted
Pinch of salt per egg white
1 teaspoon ground cinnamon

Directions

1. Preheat oven to 350° F.
2. Beat egg whites and salt at medium speed until frothy.
3. Add sugar one tablespoon at a time. Continue beating until stiff.
4. Add cinnamon and mix briefly.
4. Spread meringue over pie.
5. Bake at 350° F. until peaks are golden brown. (10-15 minutes)

Nutrition Facts		
Serving Size 20 g		
Amount Per Serving		
Calories 29		Calories from Fat 0
		% Daily Value*
Total Fat 0.0g		0%
Trans Fat 0.0g		
Cholesterol 0mg		0%
Sodium 40mg		2%
Total Carbohydrates 6.0g		2%
Protein 1.4g		
Vitamin A 0%	*	Vitamin C 0%
Calcium 0%	*	Iron 0%
Nutrition Grade C+		
* Based on a 2000 calorie diet		

White shelled eggs are produced by hens with white feathers and ear lobes. Brown shelled eggs are produced by hens with red feathers and ear lobes. The nutrition of brown and white eggs is the same.

Cardamom Meringue Topping

- A unique spice addition.
- Tops 9-inch pie.
- Serves: 8

Ingredients

3 egg whites
6 tablespoons confectioners' sugar, sifted
Pinch of salt per egg white
1 teaspoon ground cardamom

Directions

1. Preheat oven to 350° F.
2. Beat egg whites and salt at medium speed until frothy.
3. Add sugar one tablespoon at a time. Continue beating until stiff.
4. Add cardamom and mix briefly.
4. Spread meringue over pie.
5. Bake at 350° F. until peaks are golden brown. (10-15 minutes)

Nutrition Facts

Serving Size 20 g

Amount Per Serving

Calories 29	Calories from Fat 0

% Daily Value*

	% Daily Value*
Total Fat 0.0g	0%
Cholesterol 0mg	0%
Sodium 40mg	2%
Total Carbohydrates 5.9g	2%
Protein 1.4g	

Vitamin A 0%	•	Vitamin C 0%
Calcium 0%	•	Iron 0%

Nutrition Grade C+

* Based on a 2000 calorie diet

The name meringue came from a pastry chef named Gasparini in the Swiss town of Merhrinyghen.

Cocoa Meringue Topping

- Chocolate cocoa taste.
- Tops 9-inch pie.
- Serves: 8

Ingredients

3 egg whites
6 tablespoons confectioners' sugar, sifted
Pinch of salt per egg white
1 teaspoon cocoa powder

Directions

1. Preheat oven to 350° F.
2. Beat egg whites and salt at medium speed until frothy.
3. Add sugar one tablespoon at a time. Continue beating until stiff.
4. Add cocoa powder and mix briefly.
4. Spread meringue over pie.
5. Bake at 350° F. until peaks are golden brown. (10-15 minutes)

Nutrition Facts

Serving Size 20 g

Amount Per Serving

Calories 29		Calories from Fat 0

	% Daily Value*
Total Fat 0.1g	**0%**
Cholesterol 0mg	**0%**
Sodium 40mg	**2%**
Total Carbohydrates 5.8g	**2%**
Protein 1.4g	

Vitamin A 0%	*	Vitamin C 0%
Calcium 0%	*	Iron 0%

Nutrition Grade C+

* Based on a 2000 calorie diet

Soaking your hands in Key lime juice and warm water once a month softens cuticles and whitens nails.

Nutmeg Meringue Topping

- Strong nutmeg flavor.
- Tops 9-inch pie.
- Serves: 8

Ingredients

3 egg whites
6 tablespoons confectioners' sugar, sifted
Pinch of salt per egg white
1 teaspoon ground nutmeg

Nutrition Facts

Serving Size 20 g

Amount Per Serving	
Calories 30	Calories from Fat 1

	% Daily Value*
Total Fat 0.1g	0%
Cholesterol 0mg	0%
Sodium 40mg	2%
Total Carbohydrates 5.9g	2%
Protein 1.4g	

Vitamin A 0%	•	Vitamin C 0%
Calcium 0%	•	Iron 0%

Nutrition Grade C+

* Based on a 2000 calorie diet

Directions

1. Preheat oven to 350° F.
2. Beat egg whites and salt at medium speed until frothy.
3. Add sugar one tablespoon at a time. Continue beating until stiff.
4. Add nutmeg and mix briefly.
4. Spread meringue over pie.
5. Bake at 350° F. until peaks are golden brown. (10-15 minutes)

Marie Antoinette is said to have prepared meringue with her own hands at the Trianon in France.

Vanilla Meringue Topping

- Slight vanilla kick.
- Tops 9-inch pie.
- Serves: 8

Ingredients

3 egg whites
6 tablespoons confectioners' sugar, sifted
Pinch of salt per egg white
½ teaspoon vanilla extract

Nutrition Facts

Serving Size 20 g

Amount Per Serving	
Calories 29	Calories from Fat 0

	% Daily Value*
Total Fat 0.0g	0%
Cholesterol 0mg	0%
Sodium 40mg	2%
Total Carbohydrates 5.8g	2%
Protein 1.4g	

Vitamin A 0%	•	Vitamin C 0%
Calcium 0%	•	Iron 0%

Nutrition Grade D
* Based on a 2000 calorie diet

Directions

1. Preheat oven to 350° F.
2. Beat egg whites and salt at medium speed until frothy.
3. Add sugar one tablespoon at a time. Continue beating until stiff.
4. Fold in vanilla extract.
5. Spread meringue over pie.
6. Bake at 350° F. until peaks are golden brown. (10-15 minutes)

Poached meringues are known as snow eggs.

Almond Meringue Topping

- Added nutty taste.
- Tops 9-inch pie.
- Serves: 8

Ingredients

3 egg whites
6 tablespoons confectioners' sugar, sifted
Pinch of salt per egg white
½ teaspoon almond extract

Nutrition Facts

Serving Size 20 g

Amount Per Serving

Calories 29	Calories from Fat 0

	% Daily Value*
Total Fat 0.0g	0%
Cholesterol 0mg	0%
Sodium 40mg	2%
Total Carbohydrates 5.8g	2%
Protein 1.4g	

Vitamin A 0%	•	Vitamin C 0%
Calcium 0%	•	Iron 0%

Nutrition Grade D

* Based on a 2000 calorie diet

Directions

1. Preheat oven to 350° F.
2. Beat egg whites and salt at medium speed until frothy.
3. Add sugar one tablespoon at a time. Continue beating until stiff.
4. Fold in almond extract.
5. Spread meringue over pie.
6. Bake at 350° F. until peaks are golden brown. (10-15 minutes)

The more sugar in a meringue, the drier and stiffer the meringue will be.

Coconut Meringue Topping

- Real coconut flavor.
- Tops 9-inch pie.
- Serves: 8

Ingredients

3 egg whites
6 tablespoons confectioners' sugar, sifted
Pinch of salt per egg white
¼ cup finely chopped coconut

Directions

1. Preheat oven to 350° F.
2. Beat egg whites and salt at medium speed until frothy.
3. Add sugar one tablespoon at a time. Continue beating until stiff.
4. Fold in chopped coconut.
5. Spread meringue over pie.
6. Bake at 350° F. until peaks are golden brown. (10-15 minutes)

Nutrition Facts	
Serving Size 22 g	
Amount Per Serving	
Calories 37	Calories from Fat 8
	% Daily Value*
Total Fat 0.9g	1%
Saturated Fat 0.7g	4%
Cholesterol 0mg	0%
Sodium 40mg	2%
Total Carbohydrates 6.1g	2%
Protein 1.4g	
Vitamin A 0%	Vitamin C 0%
Calcium 0%	Iron 0%
Nutrition Grade C	
* Based on a 2000 calorie diet	

There are French, Swiss and Italian meringues. The French technique is most commonly used for Key lime pies.

Saffron Meringue Topping

- Bitter honey flavor, great with Key lime.
- Tops 9-inch pie.
- Serves: 8

Ingredients

3 egg whites
6 tablespoons confectioners' sugar, sifted
Pinch of salt per egg white
Pinch of saffron

Directions

1. Preheat oven to 350° F.
2. Beat egg whites at medium speed until frothy.
3. Add sugar one tablespoon at a time. Continue beating until stiff.
4. Fold in saffron.
5. Spread meringue over pie.
6. Bake at 350° F. until peaks are golden brown. (10-15 minutes)

Cream of tartar crystallizes out of solution when grapes are fermented during wine making. Also known as potassium bitartrate, it is a popular stabilizer for meringue.

Key Lime Zest Meringue Topping

- Added Key lime kick.
- Tops 9-inch pie.
- Serves: 8

Ingredients

3 egg whites
6 tablespoons confectioners' sugar, sifted
Pinch of salt per egg white
Zest of one Key lime

Nutrition Facts	
Serving Size 28 g	
Amount Per Serving	
Calories 31	Calories from Fat 0
	% Daily Value*
Total Fat 0.0g	**0%**
Cholesterol 0mg	**0%**
Sodium 40mg	**2%**
Total Carbohydrates 6.6g	**2%**
Protein 1.4g	
Vitamin A 0%	Vitamin C 4%
Calcium 0%	Iron 0%
Nutrition Grade C+	
* Based on a 2000 calorie diet	

Directions

1. Preheat oven to 350° F.
2. Beat egg whites and salt at medium speed until frothy.
3. Add sugar one tablespoon at a time. Continue beating until stiff.
4. Fold in Key lime zest.
5. Spread meringue over pie.
6. Bake at 350° F. until peaks are golden brown. (10-15 minutes)

Eggs contain the highest quality food protein known. It is second only to mother's milk for human nutrition.

Alternative Recipes

Low Fat Key Lime Pie

- Lower in fat.
- Serves: 8

Nutrition Facts
Serving Size 88 g
Amount Per Serving
Calories 169   Calories from Fat 4
% Daily Value*
Total Fat 0.5g   1%
Trans Fat 0.0g
Cholesterol 0mg   0%
Sodium 184mg   8%
Total Carbohydrates 34.5g   12%
Sugars 31.4g
Protein 8.1g
Vitamin A 11%   •   Vitamin C 0%
Calcium 20%   •   Iron 4%
Nutrition Grade B
* Based on a 2000 calorie diet

Ingredients

2 cups fat free soda cracker crumbs
4 tablespoons fat free butter alternative
1/8 cup water
1 14 ounce can fat free sweetened condensed milk
¾ cup egg substitute
½ cup Key lime juice

Directions

1. Preheat oven to 350° F.
2. Combine soda crackers, butter alternative and water. Mix until coated.
3. Press into 9-inch pie pan and bake at 350° F. for 8 minutes.
4. Combine sweetened condensed milk and eggs. Mix well.
5. Slowly incorporate Key lime juice.
6. Pour mixture into prepared crust. Chill well before serving.

" I don't want to spend my life not having good food going into my pie hole. That hole was made for pies."

— Paula Dean

Low Sugar Key Lime Pie

- Check individual dietary requirements!
- Tasty low-sugar alternative.
- Serves: 8

Ingredients

1 ½ cups plain graham cracker crumbs

6 tablespoons butter or diet butter, melted

1 tablespoon Splenda®

8 ounces fat free cream cheese

16 oz fat free sour cream

¼ cup Key lime juice

1 cup crushed pineapple

Nutrition Facts

Serving Size 128 g

Amount Per Serving

Calories 211   Calories from Fat 127

% Daily Value*

Total Fat 14.1g   **22%**

Saturated Fat 7.5g   **37%**

Trans Fat 0.0g

Cholesterol 36mg   **12%**

Sodium 214mg   **9%**

Total Carbohydrates 15.3g   **5%**

Dietary Fiber 0.5g   **2%**

Sugars 6.5g

Protein 4.2g

Vitamin A 22%   •   Vitamin C 15%

Calcium 10%   •   Iron 3%

Nutrition Grade C-

* Based on a 2000 calorie diet

Directions

1. Preheat oven to 350° F.
2. Combine first three ingredients and press firmly into 9-inch pie pan.
2. Bake at 350° F. for 8 – 10 minutes.
3. Let cream cheese soften. Beat until smooth.
4. Add sour cream. Continue mixing.
5. Add Key lime juice. Continue mixing.
6. Fold in pineapple. Pour into prepared shell.
7. Chill before serving.

Gluten Free Key Lime Pie

- Check individual products!
- Check individual dietary requirements!
- Serves: 8

Ingredients

4 tablespoons butter, melted
2 tablespoons agave nectar
1 ½ cups almond flour
½ teaspoon salt
1 teaspoon cinnamon
3 egg yolks
1 14 ounce can non-fat sweetened condensed milk
½ cup Key lime juice

Directions

1. Preheat oven to 350° F.
2. Combine butter, agave, flour, salt and cinnamon.
3. Press into greased 9-inch pie pan. Bake for 10 – 12 minutes until golden.
4. Combine sweetened condensed milk and eggs. Mix well.
5. Slowly incorporate Key lime juice.
6. Pour mixture into prepared crust.
7. Bake at 350° F for 8-10 minutes.
8. Chill before serving.

Nutrition Facts

Serving Size 89 g

Amount Per Serving	
Calories 241	Calories from Fat 91

	% Daily Value*
Total Fat 10.1g	16%
Saturated Fat 4.5g	22%
Trans Fat 0.0g	
Cholesterol 94mg	31%
Sodium 262mg	11%
Total Carbohydrates 33.3g	11%
Dietary Fiber 0.7g	3%
Sugars 31.9g	
Protein 7.2g	

Vitamin A 8%	•	Vitamin C 0%
Calcium 21%	•	Iron 2%

Nutrition Grade D+

* Based on a 2000 calorie diet

Vegan Key Lime Pie

- Check individual dietary requirements!
- Serves: 8

Ingredients

1 cup shredded coconut
1 cup pecans
½ cup Medjool dates, pitted
16 ounces non-dairy cream cheese
1 cup sugar
1 teaspoon vanilla extract
¼ cup Key lime juice
Zest of one Key lime
2 tablespoons cornstarch

Nutrition Facts

Serving Size 111 g

Amount Per Serving

Calories 295   Calories from Fat 118

% Daily Value*

Total Fat 13.1g	**20%**
Saturated Fat 3.8g	**19%**
Trans Fat 0.0g	
Cholesterol 5mg	**2%**
Sodium 352mg	**15%**
Total Carbohydrates 36.3g	**12%**
Dietary Fiber 2.5g	**10%**
Sugars 30.1g	
Protein 8.4g	

Vitamin A 17% • Vitamin C 1%
Calcium 26% • Iron 4%

Nutrition Grade D+

* Based on a 2000 calorie diet

Directions

1. Preheat oven to 350° F.
2. Blend coconut and pecans until coarse.
3. Add dates and blend until ingredients stick together.
4. Form into 9-inch pie pan. Freeze for 20 minutes.
5. Combine cream cheese, sugar, vanilla, Key lime juice, zest and cornstarch.
6. Mix until smooth.
7. Pour mixture into crust and bake for 30 minutes.
8. Let cool. Refrigerate and garnish with fresh fruit before serving.

White House Key Lime Pie

- Created by Chef Bill Yosses, White House
- Lower in fat and sugar
- Serves: 8

Ingredients

1 cup graham cracker crumbs

1 tablespoon sugar

4 tablespoons unsalted butter, melted

1 ½ cups Greek yogurt

4 large egg yolks

½ cup Key lime juice

2 tablespoons honey

1/3 cup granulated sugar

whipped cream

Nutrition Facts

Serving Size 43 g

Amount Per Serving

Calories 179	Calories from Fat 81

	% Daily Value*
Total Fat 9.0g	14%
Saturated Fat 4.5g	22%
Trans Fat 0.0g	
Cholesterol 120mg	40%
Sodium 139mg	6%
Total Carbohydrates 23.2g	8%
Dietary Fiber 0.7g	3%
Sugars 16.3g	
Protein 2.1g	

Vitamin A 6%	•	Vitamin C 0%
Calcium 1%	•	Iron 4%

Nutrition Grade D+

* Based on a 2000 calorie diet

Directions

1. Preheat oven to 350° F.

2. Stir graham cracker crumbs, sugar, and butter in a bowl until combined. Then press mixture evenly into bottom and up the sides of a 9" pie plate.

3. Bake crust 10 minutes then remove from oven to cool.

4. Whisk together yogurt, egg yolks, honey, and sugar; add juice and whisk until well combined.

5. Pour filling into crust, and bake for 20 minutes in 350°F oven (mixture will not be firm).

6. Cool and refrigerate overnight.

Garnishing Tips & Tricks

Garnishing is a great way to make your pie stand above the rest. From the French *garnir* meaning *to adorn*, garnish can be anything that decorates your pie when it is served. Entire books have been written about the art and techniques of garnishing, but it need not be complicated. You can create beautiful accents for your pie by following a few basic guidelines.

- **What to use:** Garnish with an ingredient that is already in your pie. For a mint cookie crust, cut cookies into half-moons and set them in the topping of each slice. Nut crust? Blend more nuts and coat the perimeter of the pie. Your sauce and topping are actually garnishes, but you can amp the appearance with some carefully placed ingredients. A fail-proof garnish on every Key lime pie is a slice of fresh Key lime or a twisted peel. Most zesters have a peeling utility so you can twist up the peel like a pro.

- **Size Matters:** Don't overdo it with your garnish. The goal is to accent the pie and its flavors – not to overwhelm. A single berry or mint leaf on a slice of pie creates better visual appeal and taste. Sprinkle chocolate or nuts close to the crust instead of covering the entire pie. Your Key Lime pie is the star of this show. It doesn't mind company, but it doesn't like to be overshadowed.

- **Color:** Bright colors make a great initial impact, and when it comes to color, fruit is your friend. Red, yellow and green fruits have the strongest impact with Key lime pie. Also consider the color of your serving plate and how well it goes with your presentation.

- **Shape:** Go round when you garnish a Key lime pie. The pie slice should have sharp, angular edges and we want to create contrast. Think twists, twirls, circles, balls and curves. You will find they exist naturally in many of the items you use to garnish.

- **Presentation:** Garnish with care. Plate one piece of pie and play around with the sauce, topping and garnish until you find a combination you are happy with. Garnish is much easier to place than it is to remove and you don't want to end up with dents, drips or spills on your pie. Be sure to wipe drips and spills from the serving plate too. Serve the test plate to yourself after everyone else is served. They will be caught up in their own pie and won't notice a thing.

- **Rise to the occasion:** If you are making the pie for a special occasion, theme your garnish around it. Garnish doesn't always have to be edible, so long as you are there to let people know what not to eat. Number shaped candles are great for birthdays, fresh flowers for romantic occasions or tropical themes. I've even used a ceramic baby as a centerpiece on a pie when friends had their first child. Candy corns for Halloween, candy hearts for Valentine's Day, Peeps® for Easter. The possibilities are endless and most people appreciate the extra effort.

- **Great Garnishes:** Almonds, pecans, walnuts, blueberries, raspberries, strawberries, Key lime slices, wedges, zest and peels, cookies, cereals, chocolate chips, mint leaves. Let your imagination run wild.

Kenny Chesney serves Key lime pie to an adoring fan at Jimmy Buffet's Margaritaville in Key West. The song *Key Lime Pie* appeared on his 2005 album, *Be As You Are*. Photo: Rob O'Neal

Serving Tips & Tricks

A Chef who was big on food presentation trained me. 'Presentation is everything," he would tell me. Taste, texture and temperate are equally important, but when it's time to serve your pie there is little that can be done to change those. I've found through the years that a great presentation can turn a good pie into a brilliant pie. Try these tips with your pie and you will see what I mean.

The Buildup: Don't wait until the last minute to mention your pie. Mention a great recipe you stumbled upon hours, days, even weeks in advance. Plant the seed about your incredible Key lime pie and it will start to grow. If you are serving the pie after a meal, invite the pie to dinner with comments such as, "I'd really love seconds, but I've just got to save room for that Key lime pie."

The Suspense: Suspense works best with buildup. Tell a little story about your pie, the recipe, or an experience you had in the Florida Keys. Ask if everyone is ready for pie, then stall. Freshen people's beverages. Tell another story. Work your way back to the kitchen slowly.

The Preparation: Presenting the pie whole is great for certain occasions, but I get more bang for my buck with each slice individually plated and lovingly decorated. Slicing and serving your pie at the table can present complications and technical problems that are easier to solve in the kitchen without a crowd. Some crusts crumble or flake apart, some fillings ooze, some knives refuse to cut. Prepare each plate in the kitchen for a slice that appears perfect every time.

The Delivery: Come up with a name for your pie. Use the naming chart in this book if you need ideas. Bring the plates to the table as if you just discovered sunken treasure. Your enthusiasm will be contagious. Serve yourself last, mention to everyone how excited you are about the pie and invite them to dig in.

The Satisfaction: Don't be afraid to toot your own horn. Mmmms, aaaaahs, extended yums and wows should get things rolling. Don't be afraid to say you even outdid yourself this time.

Damage Control: Is your pie a disaster? It's very hard to mess up a Key lime pie, but life is full of variables. Should you experience one of those rare occasions that the pie is a disaster, blame me and invite everyone to the kitchen for margaritas.

Caught in the act!
Marbles the cat couldn't resist checking out the latest Key lime creation. Never leave your Key lime pie unattended, or you are likely to find someone has been sticking their fingers (or paws) in your pie, unable to resist the sweet Key lime taste. Photo courtesy of Rob O'Neal.

Naming Your Pie

Anybody can serve Key lime pie. Add to the allure of yours by giving it a name worthy of the Florida Keys. Choose from the words below and combine them with your pie's main flavors and textures to create names like 'Hemingway's Rum Crunch Key Lime Pie.'

People
Ernest Hemingway
Tennessee Williams
Mel Fisher
Captain Tony
Henry Flagler
Jimmy Buffett
President Truman
Shel Silverstein

Places
Ocean Reef
Islamorada
Key Largo
Mile Marker Zero
Southernmost Point
Fort Jefferson
Dry Tortugas
7-Mile Bridge
Cow Key Channel
Mallory Square

Streets
Greene Street
Duval Street
Love Lane
Simonton Street
Overseas Highway
Card Sound Road
Eaton Street
Peacon Lane

And More
Pirate's
Wrecker's
Captain's
Smuggler's
Admiral's
Sunset
Hurricane
Water Spout
Speakeasy
Voodoo

Misc.
Aunt Sally
William Curry
Sponge Fisherman's
Chris Columbus
Conch Key
Island City
Cayo Hueso
Bone Island
End of the Road
Havana
Green Flash
Shotgun Shack
Cock Fighter's
Atocha
Vandenberg
Pennekamp
Fat Albert
Fantasy Fest
Wharf
Seaport

Tennessee Williams enjoys Key lime pie on a Key West beach. LOOK Magazine Photograph Collection, Library of Congress, Prints & Photographs Division, [Reproduction number e.g., LC-L9-60-8812, frame 8].

Secret Ingredients

Secret ingredients add to the mystique of any pie. People want what they can't have. Secret ingredients are like magic tricks. They are magical, as long as the magician is the only one who knows the secret. Keep this in mind when mentioning your own secret ingredient. Much like a magic trick, revelation of the secret will give a moment of satisfaction followed by letdown.

- The first secret ingredient in your Key lime pie should be quality. Use the best ingredients possible. They make a difference. People are served average food at restaurants on a regular basis. Fresh, top of the line products will make a difference they can taste but can't place.

- Secret ingredients should be flavorful, but subtle. Use just enough of the ingredient to peak curiosity. Peanut Butter wouldn't be a secret ingredient in a Peanut Butter Key Lime Pie, but a dash of cocoa or cappuccino powder can be familiar and delightful, but hard to name.

- Chose a secret ingredient that compliments the pie you are preparing. Many of the recipes here already have a secret ingredient included. Keep it to yourself and it becomes your secret ingredient.

- Don't be afraid to experiment. It's hard to screw up a Key lime pie. Go through your spice rack, refrigerator and pantry. When you come across something unique, adapt the recipe and mix a little in. Just keep in mind that less is more when experimenting.

- Some people have allergies to certain foods or strict dietary guidelines. Don't keep your secret from them, but insist they keep it from others.

- The best secret ingredients are passion and love. Use them in every pie you make and you will see the difference.

The following ingredients have worked great as 'secrets' in my Key lime pies. Try them out with recipes that don't already include that ingredient and make them your own. Some work better with crusts, others with fillings, and each to personal taste. Experiment and have fun.

Cinnamon	Ice Cream	Nuts
Cardamom	Cocoa	Peanut Butter
Cayenne Pepper	Chocolate	Yoohoo®
Nutmeg	Coffee or Espresso	Orange Juice
Saffron	Baileys® Irish Cream	Agave
All Spice	Kahlua® Coffee Liquor	Apple Sauce
Anise	Rum	Sour Cream
Fennel	Coconut	Avocado
Ginger	Vanilla (and other extracts)	Honey
Mint	Flavored Tea	Maple Syrup
Lemon Grass	Hot Sauce	Tropical Fruits
Key Lime Zest	Cookies	Yogurt
Lemon Zest	Cereals	Pretzels
Poppy Seed	Carmel	Marshmallows
Salt	Butterscotch	Fresh Berries

Key Lime Pie Chart

Track your favorite pie combinations here.

CRUST	FILLING	COOKING	TOPPING	SAUCE

Key Lime Pie Chart

CRUST	FILLING	COOKING	TOPPING	SAUCE

Notes:

Notes:

Notes:

Notes:

In Closing: Just Desserts

Some people were enraged at the mere mention of a Key lime pie cookbook. "There's only one way to make a real Key lime pie!" "This is sacrilege!" "Your variations are an abomination to the dessert!" It is safe to say religion and politics are not the only things that get people heated.

My journey to find the ultimate Key lime pie had me floating on Cloud Nine. I was thrilled with the discovery of each fun fact. A new joy accompanied every morsel of pie history I uncovered. The discovery of a new ingredient left me feeling like a kid in a candy store anxious to try it out and share with friends.

My goal with *The Key Lime Pie Cookbook* is not to judge right from wrong in the Key lime community or argue opinions on who has the best pie in town. My goal is simply to share. Share my favorite Key lime pie recipes, share the fascinating history behind the pie, share some fun facts and old wives tales about the fruit and share the excitement it has brought.

Key lime pie is a special no matter how you slice it. I hope you enjoy creating these Key lime pies as much as I do. If you enjoy the book, tell your friends or write a five star review. If you think it needs something, let me know and I'll try to include it in a future edition. If you hated the book, shoot me an e-mail and I'll make things better. After all, it's just desserts.

Luck & Limes!
david@phantompress.com

Former Florida Governor Bob Graham is shown serving Key Lime pie during "Conch Day" celebrations in 1983 in this photo from The State Archives of Florida.

Acknowledgements

A team of chefs celebrate their latest creations in this 1949 photo from the Spottswood Collection of The State Archives of Florida.

Thank You!

Research: Tom Hambright, Paul Menta, D.O. Christian Rieger, Jerry Wilkinson, surveys conducted by The American Pie Council®, Crisco®, and Four Points by Sheraton®.

Photos: Rob O'Neal, Nick Doll, Monroe County Public Library Archives & State Archives of Florida.

Key Lime Kirby: Dan Schwab

Publicity: Carol Shaughnessy, Stacey Mitchell, Andy Newman, Molly O'Neill, Epicurious, Steve Garbarino, The Wall Street Journal, The American Pie Council, The Food Network's Food Challenge, Victoria Allman, Rob O'Neal, Larry Bradley, Kate Miano, Erika Biddle, Michael Marrero, Marky Pierson, Bill Hoebee, Loretta-Maria Adkins, Mandy Miles, Terry Schmida, Joanne Schmida, The Porch, Vino's, The Chart Room, Abigail's Chili Cook Off, The Key West Citizen, Chad Newman, Steve Panariello & Digital Island Media.

Editing: Mandy Miles

Contributors, Recipe Testers & Tasters: Heather-May Potter, Tim Schwarz, Melissa Clarke, Chris Shultz, Rob Marjerison, Tim Watson, Dorothy Drennen, Joel Biddle, Liz Weinstock, Brett, Stephanie & Blake Southgate, The Flagg Family, Laura & Jim Thornbrugh, Eli & Kenna Pancamo, Erin McKenna, The Porter Family of Nebraska, Joy Clark Long, Tim Madison, Ralph Ballentine, John Nolte, Gregg McGrady, Alan Nelson, William Ellis, Stan Miles, Charles Belanger, Mike Marrero, Liz Love, Renee Spencer, The Curry Mansion, Joe McGuire, Jimmy & Susan Weekley, Ann & Jorge Marrero, Frank Holden, Jean & Joe Thornton.

Special Thanks: Heather-May Potter, Tod, Eileene & Kristin Sloan.

PHANTOM **PRESS**
KEY WEST

MORE BOOKS BY DAVID L. SLOAN

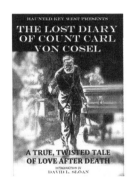

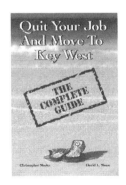

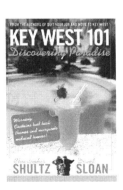

About The Author

David L. Sloan landed his first baking job at 16 and continued his career in the industry with a Hospitality Management degree from Florida International University. During this time he apprenticed under South Florida Chef of the Year, Pascal Oudin at the Coral Gables Colonnade Hotel before relocating to the Atlantic Ocean where he served as General Manager for Premier Cruise Lines.

Sloan moved to Key West in 1996 and rediscovered his love of baking after stumbling upon a Key lime pie recipe at the Curry Mansion. He bought an old citrus grove where he lived for eight months, has served as judge for the commercial division of the *Great American Pie Festival*, competed in the professional division at *The National Pie Championships* and filmed with the *Food Network's Food Challenge*.

David is a member of the *National Pie Council* and the author of a dozen books, for which he has been featured on The History Channel, Travel Channel, Discovery Channel, Food Network and more. He is also the co-founder of The Key Lime Festival and holds a record for the world's largest Key Lime Pie.

Young women pose for photographs during the 1953 Key Lime Festival in Key Largo, Florida. Publication info: Byrum, Joanne / Sweeting, Jackie /Smith, Carolyn /Kaufman, Barbara /Albury, Dorothy. Uncle Johnny. Source: State Archives of Florida.

37959947R00104

Made in the USA
Charleston, SC
24 January 2015